SOLDIERS' *Tales* #2

A collection of true stories from Aussie Soldiers

Big Sky Publishing Pty Ltd
PO Box 303, Newport, NSW 2106, Australia
Phone: 1300 364 611
Fax: (61 2) 9918 2396
Email: info@bigskypublishing.com.au
Web: www.bigskypublishing.com.au

Cover design and typesetting: Think Productions

National Library of Australia Cataloguing-in-Publication entry (pbk)
Title: Soliders tales. 2 : a collection of true stories from Aussie soldiers / Denny Neave.
ISBN: 9781921941795 (pbk.)
Subjects: Australia. Army--Military life.
          Australia. Army--History.
          Soldiers--Australia--Anecdotes.
Other Authors/Contributors: Neave, Denny, 1970-
Dewey Number: 355.0092294

National Library of Australia Cataloguing-in-Publication entry (ebook)
Title: Soliders tales. 2 : a collection of true stories from Aussie soldiers / Denny Neave.
ISBN: 9781921941856 (ebook)
Subjects: Australia. Army--Military life.
          Australia. Army--History.
          Soldiers--Australia--Anecdotes.
Other Authors/Contributors: Neave, Denny, 1970-
Dewey Number: 355.0092294
Printed in China through Bookbuilders

SOLDIERS' Tales #2

A collection of true stories from Aussie Soldiers

BIG SKY PUBLISHING
www.bigskypublishing.com.au

Edited by Denny Neave

Contents

Introduction

In 2008, after having completed research for my first book – *Aussie Soldier Up Close and Personal* – I decided that I had uncovered such a plethora of tales that had not seen the light of day, that I would stitch together a small book called *Soldiers Tales*. I sifted through the material and chose a selection of stories, quotes and anecdotes that encompass our short military history, choosing those that provide fascinating glimpses of our military service through the decades.

Several years on, and with more research under my belt, I felt the need to expand upon this first installment. Taking a slightly different tack by not wanting to put forward stories that were my choice alone, I sought the counsel of a number of my colleagues, who are more credentialed military historians than I, and asked for their *Soldiers Tales* of choice. This volume contains those tales. I have also included a few others that I found along the way.

Most of these stories and quotes are first hand. However, given the time that has elapsed and the passing of many of our veterans, I have also included some recollections from secondary sources. I regard these too as *Soldiers Tales*. Those telling them share the same passion for preserving our heritage as I do.

They grew up listening, with ears pricked, to stories told by fathers, mothers, uncles, grandfathers, etc., just as I did. And just because they have passed on a story that a relative told them does not diminish its place in the tapestry of our military history. My personal experience is that if I did not share the stories my father told me, they may never be told, and would therefore be lost for all time. If many other veterans are like my father, grandfather and great-grandfather, then they will tend to only share these stories sparingly, with trepidation and only with trusted loved ones. To lose these stories would be tragic.

I have also taken the liberty of casting the net a little wider, and have included a few morsels from allies who now call Australia home.

Most of these stories appear in print for the first time here; others have been previously published and are worthy of telling again. In the interests of authenticity, I have not changed the voices of those telling the stories, so there is an eclectic mix of language from eras past and present.

I hope you enjoy reading these stories as much as I have enjoyed finding them.

A Tearful Thank You

On one of our early Platoon patrols in South Vietnam [SVN] we were moving through light bush about a click inside the free-fire zone. Any locals found there were to be treated as Viet Cong [the enemy]. We apprehended a person who turned out to be an elderly woman. She was dressed in rags and her only possession seemed to be a small hessian bag with a few pieces of fruit in it. The Diggers formed a perimeter and passed her into Platoon HQ. Through our SVN interpreter we found that her identification was in order and she had a letter explaining that she was 'simple' – mentally incompetent – and homeless. The Diggers were watching the whole interview process, fascinated by their first view of 'the enemy'. Finally, we pointed her towards the nearest village and she started to shuffle off. However, as she passed the machine gunner, he rose and stopped her. I might add that at this point none of the Diggers knew of her 'simple' or homeless status. He handed her something. Another Digger stood and handed her something else. Then another. Soon she had a line of Diggers who, one at a time, rose, approached and handed her something. It wasn't long before she had more things than would fit in the bag. A Digger then emptied a Claymore mine out of its carry bag and gave her the bag. I could see, as she put the rest of her goodies into the cloth bag that the Diggers had given her whatever food they could spare – plus cigarettes and chocolates – anything except cans, which she couldn't have opened. It was entirely spontaneous and I was angry at myself that I hadn't started the gift-giving. By the time she left, I reckon everyone in the Platoon had contributed something, and yet not a word had been spoken, except by her in her tearful Vietnamese 'thank yous'.

Lieutenant Dave Sabben, MG,
6th Battalion the Rayal Australian Regiment, Vietnam

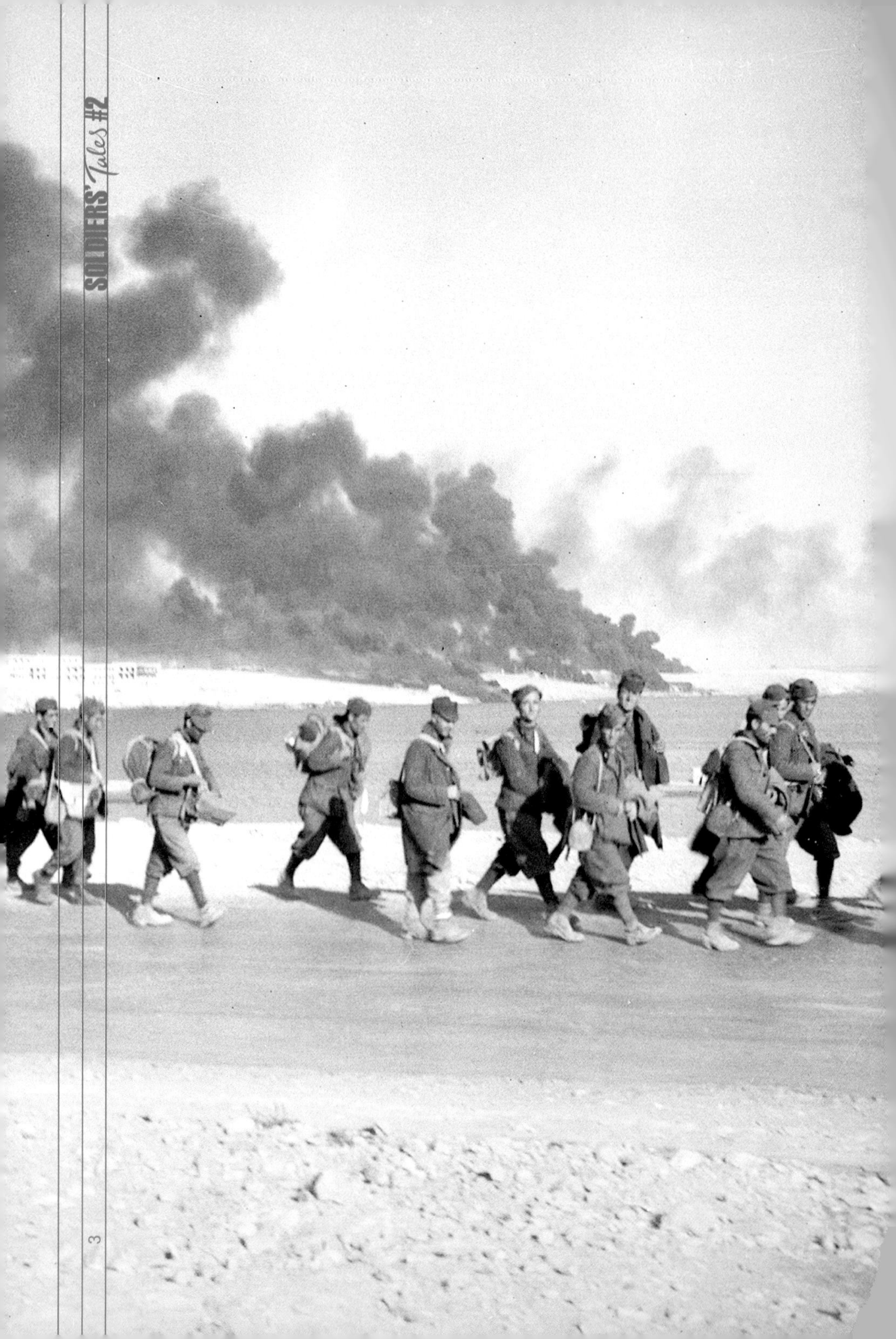

A Humble Lieutenant Captures a Commanding General in the Battle of Tobruk

Charles Granquist, 2/4th Battalion, Tobruk

On 7 January 1941, the 2/4th Battalion moved from Bardia and closed up the eastern defences of the fortress of Tobruk, taking up position in a series of wadis (gullies) which ran down to the sea. Here we were subject to constant shelling. A number of patrols were sent out to gather information on the enemy. Any movement in the open produced a torrent of fire. From the information obtained by these patrols, it was decided a more suitable position was required for an attack on the fortress. After ten long days we were relieved by the 2/5th Battalion. After a well-earned rest for the day, we were issued with new clothing and were once again on the move. We marched through the night to the southern side of Tobruk; the new location from where the attack would be made.

Early in the morning of 21 January, the 16th Brigade breached the forward defences. We moved through these breaches only to be greeted by an enormous artillery barrage courtesy of the Italians. The bombs followed all the way to the Bardia road. Shortly after crossing the road we captured the sector Headquarters at Sidi Mahmud. Here we regrouped and received orders to advance across the airfield and capture Fort Solaro, which was thought to be the location of the fortress Headquarters. We moved off at 1400 hours supported by a British field artillery regiment and other units.

Severe resistance was encountered at the aerodrome and two companies had to be diverted to deal with this. A Company pushed on to Fort Solaro but there were no signs of the Headquarters anywhere. The following account is taken from *White over Green*, the history of the 2/4th Battalion:

Lieutenant Copland, Corporal Vic Hill and Private Nobby Clarke were in a forward position when out of the gloom appeared an Italian naval officer and said:

'His Excellence wishes to surrender.'

Copland replied: 'OK bring him along.'

A very scared Italian explained that His Excellence wanted to surrender to an officer and that the surrender had to take place at his Headquarters. Eventually Copland convinced him that he was an officer and the three followed him to the escarpment where in the half light they came to a doorway cut in the rock.

All three had plenty of grenades with them and the naval officer knew, in the event of any funny business what to expect. As they approached the door several shots rang out and the Italian really put on an act when the Australians pulled out their grenades. He stopped his friends and the party went in.

The prospect inside was grim. There was a tunnel zigzagging this way and that through the soft rock with huge caverns dug out on either side. They were full of Italian soldiers. Copland left Nobby Clarke at the first turn and went on with Vic Hill and left him at another vantage point. He then went on with the naval lieutenant. Then he came on to the Headquarters itself.

Sumptuous was hardly the word. It was a huge chamber, beautifully furnished with sycamore table, bedroom suite and chairs galore. Behind the table sat His Excellency and staff. Military, Naval and Air Force attachès and a Primate of the Church, all in full regimental dress. This was no less than General Manella himself.

Lieutenant Copland feeling very grubby in front of all this finery, returned the General's salute and then had to let go of his pistol to shake the old boy's hand. This was a pathetic episode. Tears welled from his eyes. He seemed an old man, dignified, quiet and very tired. He made his formal surrender and handed over his pistol. Still very conscious of three lone Australians being entirely responsible for the General and his entourage and hundreds of Italians, Copland suggested they move out into the open. General Manella insisted on proceeding last.

Corporal Hill started the men moving and took the naval officer with him. As things were moving rather slowly, with night closing in, he asked the naval bloke the Italian words for double march. He was told ‹forte presto› which turned out to be a rather free translation. The Australians quickly took up the call with other typical Australian adjectives thrown in and the mob emerged from the hole in the wall to be greeted by other members of A Company.

Soon, all the members of the Italian staff came out followed by Copland who, tired, hoarse and relieved was helping the heartbroken Manella. So, a humble lieutenant of the 2/4th Battalion had captured the General commanding the garrison of Tobruk and accepted his surrender.

The battle of Tobruk was over and we were stood down. It was a reasonably cold night and we had no blankets but we just lay down and slept – we had been on the move and under fire for some 17 hours.

The next morning we moved into Tobruk and our platoon and a troop from 6th Division Cavalry Regiment were first into the main square where there was a flagpole from which an Italian flag was flying. Then something happened that featured in documentaries for many years after the war. The Italian flag was eagerly pulled down but we had no Australian flag to replace it. My mate 'Rusty' McWilliam got hold of a slouch hat from somewhere (we were wearing steel helmets so this was no mean feat) and tied it to the flagpole rope. He cheekily raised the Aussie slouch hat to fly proudly over the town square to the delight of every digger present. There was plenty of grog and tinned food for the taking and we celebrated heartily. Best of all, when we bedded down in some villas nearby – praise be – there were beaut showers which we made the most of.

The Last Rose of Ypres

Frank Hurley, Official War Photographer, Commonwealth Military Forces, Ypres, 1917

To drive the Boche [slang term used for the German soldiers] from Ypres, it was necessary to practically raze the town; and now that we hold it we are shelled in return, but shelling now makes little difference, for the fine buildings and churches are scarce left stone on stone. The car alighted us just near the ruins of the famous Cloth Hall. Regulations compelled it to remain without the ruins of the town. Our big guns, which are situated near the city, maintain an endless bombardment on the Boche line and trenches and shot for shot is returned. Frequently these fall short or are deliberately fired into the ruins by the Boche. Then with a deafening boom comes the explosion; bricks stones and debris fly skyward, shell splinters whiz past and then a cloud of brickdust fills the air for a few minutes and then comes another fizzing scream, and boom, boom, boom, goes on eternally. Sometimes they land on the road, sometimes on a team of horses and sometimes on a group of men. Whether they land on ruins, horses or men is a matter of comparative indifference so dulled have our susceptibilities and finer instincts have become.

Wilkins, myself and Sergeant Harrison wandered through the ruins, pathetic, though awesome in their demolition. The main roads have been cleared of most of the debris, and instead of the fine buildings that were, hideous gapings and breaches

in shot away remnants remain. In many cases the roofs and top storeys have been blown away and the fronts shorn off, so that the smashed up rooms gape into the street. In other places there are just heaps of bricks and a few standing pillars. Roaming amongst the domestic ruins made me sad. Here and there were fragments of toys; what a source of happiness they once were. Bedsteads broken and twisted almost into knots lay about, almost hidden with brick dust. A stove riddled with shrapnel, roofs poised on almost shot away walls, and walls balanced in every impossible fashion, that seemed to defy all laws of equilibrium and gravitation. Down in the cellars, quite a number of Royal Artillerymen had their billets, and it made me grin to see their cooks with funny improvised ranges, concocting stews from their army rations in some hovel which admitted as much light through the roof as the gaping walls. But most regrettable of all is the ruin of the famous Cloth Hall. This magnificent old church is now a remnant of torn walls and rubbish. The fine tower is a pitiable apology of a brick dump, scarred and riddled with shell holes. Its beautifully carved facades are 'small-poxed' with shell splinters, not a vestige of the carving having escaped. The figures are headless and the wonderful columns and carved pillars lay like fallen giants across the mangled remnants of roofs and other superstructures. Oh! It's too terrible for words. Returning to the car in the evening over the shell-cratered roads we came upon an enormous crater. God knows what did it, but pacing round the lip it measured 75 yards round, its depth about 25 to 30 feet! Then we came to a tiny courtyard, which had escaped for some time the ravages of bombardment. The strafed trees were coming back to life and budding, and there beside a great shell crater blossomed a single rose. How out of place it seemed amidst all this ravage. I took compassion on it and plucked it. The last rose of Ypres.

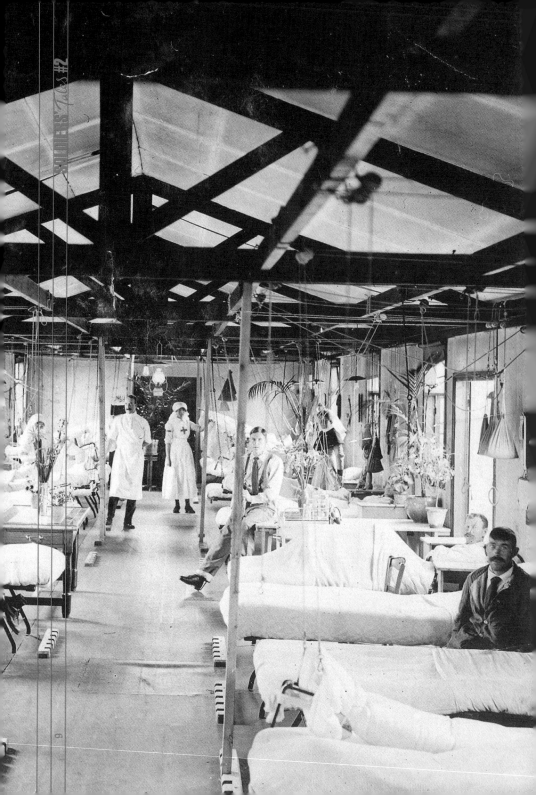

Left Out
In No Man's Land

Sister Margaret Dorothy (Dot) Edis, 2nd Australian Casualty Clearing Station

No. 2 Australian Casualty Clearing Station, France: We moved from there [Steenwerck] to Blondek and we were nicely stationed there when the retreat started. I am doing night duty and all night long on the hills behind me the lights were moving so when the orderly officer did his round at four o'clock, I said, 'Look, why are things going back to front?' 'What do you mean?' I said, 'Well you watch here, all the lights have been going the wrong way.' He said, 'How long have you noticed that?' I said, 'For the last few hours.' 'Well', he said, 'You just keep very, very quiet, say nothing.' The next thing is up comes a London bus. He said, 'Every nurse make and grab all you can in your handbag and get into that bus and out of here.' Then along comes the ambulance train and all the men and the orderlies are putting the patients on the ambulance train. We started back and as we got so many miles along the track we go through the British Tommies and we're cheered and roared at, and we find out after that there was a retreat behind us and we were left out in no man's land.

Last Men Standing

by Damien Finlayson

The 1st Australian Tunnelling Company:
Rejet-de-Beaulieu – 4 November 1918.

In March 1917, Captain Oliver Woodward of the 1st Australian Tunnelling Company (1st ATC) attended a 10-day bridge-building course the First Army Bridging School at Aire south-west of Hazebrouck. Thus trained, he was the company's natural candidate when, on 1 November 1918, three weeks after the last of the Australian infantry divisions had left the field of battle, he was instructed to construct a heavy vehicle bridge across Lock No. 1 over the Sambre-Oise Canal outside the village of Rejet-de-Beaulieu. His unit was still in action moving eastward towards Belgium with the British Fourth Army. In those last days of the war, the British 1st Division found its pursuit of the retreating Germans but held up by the Sambre-Oise Canal.

The usual bridge over the canal in the village had been destroyed and the Germans had dug in on the eastern side. Just to the north of the old bridge was the lock where the canal was only 6 metres wide. While the top of the lock gates offered a means of crossing the canal, this could only be done one man at a time. To make matters worse, a German machine gun post had been established among three buildings on the far side of the canal.

Captain Woodward therefore, along with Lieutenants Archie Thomson, Stan Sawyer and 95 other ranks from No. 4 Section of the 1st ATC reported to the 1st Division's 409th Company, Royal Engineers under the command of Major George Findlay, in readiness for an assault on the canal by the British 2nd Infantry Brigade.

The British engineers had the job of constructing infantry and light transport bridges. The Australians had to construct a heavy traffic, tank bridge after the infantry attack, which was scheduled to commence at 5.45 am, 4 November.

While the men could not know that the Armistice was only one week away, they knew it was imminent. A sense of dread and anxiety gripped each of them and each silently wondered if, after all they had been through, they would be finally denied the joy of safety and a home-coming when its promise was so close to hand. Corporal Albert Davey was one of those chosen to participate in the attack. When he heard this and so sure was he that he would not survive, he insisted that Captain Woodward take possession of his personal belongings and send them to his wife. This was a man whom Capt Woodward had always regarded as being cool-headed. In spite of his dread conviction, Albert Davey did not shirk his duty and joined the bridging party.

On the night of the 3–4 November, the party crept forward with its load of girders as a storm of artillery raged overhead. After the start of the infantry attack awaiting their order to commence construction, the Australians had to lie in wait within 300 metres of the lock with their load of bridge sections, in the dark and under artillery fire in what shell craters and hand-dug holes they could find.

As the attack commenced, Oliver Woodward with one of his most trusted men, Staff Sergeant Hector Hutchinson, crept forward to determine the situation at the canal. In the gathering light, they watched Major Findlay cross the lock gates and lead a bombing raid on the German machine gun located in the houses opposite the lock. The 409th Field Company began to suffer casualties including the major who was wounded. Major Findlay carried on, commanding the successful completion of the light bridges across the canal. For his part the Major won a Victoria Cross to add to his two Military Crosses. Oliver Woodward, seeing the casualties suffered by the British engineers, offered the assistance of his men, an offer that was readily accepted. It was not until 7.30 am that Major Findlay ordered the Australians to begin the construction of their tank bridge. Two hours later and despite the heavily shelling still going on around, the bridge was completed and the British attack carried forward – the canal was taken that day and a week later the war ended with the canal many kilometres behind the frontline.

Albert Davies, who had a premonition of his death, was indeed killed. Also killed were Sappers Arthur Johnson, Charles Barrett and Fred Knight with another five sappers wounded. For their past, Lieutenants Archie Thomson and Stan Sawyer were awarded the Military Cross while Staff Sergeant Hector Hutchinson, who assisted with the capture of a German machine-gun in addition to his work with the bridge construction, was awarded the Distinguished Conduct Medal.

Archie Thomson, whom Oliver Woodward described as a 'Scotsman of the fire-eating type', was later also awarded the Distinguished Conduct Medal in recognition for this outstanding service during his time as a non-commissioned officer. Although there were several tunnellers who crossed the divide between 'other ranks' and 'officers' during their time in active service, he was the only officer in the Australian Tunnelling companies to be decorated as both a commissioned and non-commissioned officer. He had only been promoted to the rank of lieutenant two months prior to the crossing of the Sambre-Oise Canal. As a sergeant, he had his right hand almost blown off during a German attack at Hill 60 in early November 1916 and he was evacuated to hospital in England. After being discharged and ordered to a base camp in England, he deserted and returned to France intent on rejoining his company. He managed to make it to the rest town of Poperinghe before being arrested by the Military Police. After hearing of this Major James Henry, the commanding officer the 1st ATC at the time, intervened and obtained permission for him to rejoin the unit.

By way of recognition of the ferocious conditions under which the men performed their duty, immediate Military Medals were also awarded to Sergeant William Field, Corporals Francis Armstrong and John Kearns, 2nd Corporals Thomas Arniguet and Harry Wilson and Sappers James Mobbs, Guerinio Quadrio, Edward Sabine, James Savage, John Temple and Thomas Walton.

Finally, Captain Oliver Woodward was awarded a second bar to his Military Cross. In so doing, he became one of only five Australian officers of the First World War to win three Military Crosses.

Of the 98 men from the 1st ATC who went into action at Rejet-de-Beaulieu, nine were made casualties and fifteen were awarded medals for gallantry. The honours awarded to those men, only one week before Armistice, were among the last handful of awards won in action by the entire Australian Imperial Force in the First World War and certainly the largest number awarded for a single action by an Australian unit in the days leading up to Armistice. Sadly, the sappers killed on 4 November 1918 were to be among the last half dozen Australians killed in action during the war. It was also a fitting end to the war that Oliver Woodward, the tunnelling companies' first Military Cross winner in July 1916, was also among the last handful of men to be awarded the same medal, not only among the Australian tunnellers, but among the whole Australian Imperial Force.

Anzac Day in Baghdad

Colonel Marcus Fielding, Iraq 2008-2009

Anzac Day is the most significant day in our military calendar. I know that members of the Australian Defence Force deployed to Iraq have observed Anzac Day over the last six years. But since only the embeds and the security detachment are left in Iraq, I decide that someone has to take the lead and start organising something.

My own knowledge of Australian military history tells me that Australian units were part of the Allied forces that operated in Mesopotamia during World War I, and I wonder how many Australian servicemen are buried here in Iraq. I am surprised to discover from the Commonwealth War Graves Commission staff that no fewer than 63 Australian and 14 New Zealand servicemen are buried in this land.

Having been in Baghdad for several months, I decide it's time I located the Baghdad War Cemetery. With some effort, I find out it's in the northern part of the city in the district of Rusafa and was first opened in April 1917.

In 1914, Baghdad was the site of the headquarters of the Turkish Army in Mesopotamia. Baghdad was also the ultimate objective of the Mesopotamian Expeditionary Force 'D', which captured the capital in March 1917. The British lost around 30,000 men fighting the Ottoman Turks and their German advisers in the Mesopotamian campaign. Over 4,000 Commonwealth casualties of World War I are commemorated by name in the Baghdad War Cemetery, many of them on special memorials.

Forty-one Australian and seven New Zealand servicemen are buried at the Baghdad War Cemetery. The more I learn about their history, the more I believe that they deserve their own commemoration ceremony at the cemetery on Anzac Day. I write a short proposal paper and pass it to Brigadier Simon Gould for his consideration. He likes the idea and we agree to a do a reconnaissance, heading out a few days later to inspect the site.

The first step in visiting any place in Baghdad is borrowing a security detachment. With two armoured Humvees escorting 'the limo', an armour-plated Chevrolet Suburban, we roll out of Victory Base and drive up Route Irish into the Green Zone. After a further 20 minutes working our way across the city, we turn a corner and the cemetery comes into view through the greenish tint of the car windows. The convoy pulls up and we jump out. We head towards a building that sits in the grounds of the cemetery and we meet Jasim.

Through our interpreter, we learn that Jasim is the caretaker and has been looking after the cemetery for the last five years. He tells us that he can't recall any Australians visiting the cemetery during his tenure as caretaker.

As we walk through the entranceway, I have one overriding impression – it's all brown. Brown dirt, brown stone headstones, brown sage bushes growing between the rows of headstones, a few small, brown stone memorials among the headstones, brown dust in the air and brown dogs lazing in the brown dirt. There is garbage everywhere. Almost all the headstones close to the entranceway are smashed.

As I continue along, a central walkway becomes discernable only because of the rows of sick-looking palm trees on either side. A pair of makeshift soccer goals has been erected. We wander slowly through the rows of headstones, reading the names as we pass. We see British, Indian, Australian, New Zealand and Polish servicemen, and the odd civilian. Several headstones simply say 'Four Soldiers of the Great War'.

We circle back towards the central part of the cemetery and inspect a squat, brown building. It turns out to be the mausoleum of Lieutenant General Sir Stanley Maude, Commander of Allied forces in Mesopotamia. His sarcophagus on the floor is simply inscribed 'Maude'. It seems an underwhelming place for a figure of such historical importance to be resting, his mausoleum now an island of stone in a sea of dirt, rubbish and dogs. The same applies to all these brave servicemen, so far from the homes they left. I wonder what their relatives would think if they could see what we see now.

Jasim tells us that he is contracted by the Commonwealth War Graves Commission, paid $300 a month to secure the cemetery, and provided with a small house in a corner of the cemetery grounds. It's just enough to ensure there is no further damage to the cemetery.

As we prepare to leave I thank Jasim for his efforts in looking after the cemetery and for allowing us to visit. I press US$50 into his palm and ask him to keep looking after our brothers. At first he refuses my gift, but eventually relents and accepts the money. We learn that Jasim is a Judo champion who has represented Iraq in international Judo competitions. As we drive back to Victory Base, we share our impressions of what was a sobering visit. Despite the difficulties, our resolve to conduct a dawn service at the cemetery on Anzac Day has firmed.

As we picked our way through the browned headstones, we noticed three gravestones that stood out from the others. These headstones bore the crest of the Royal Australian Navy (RAN). The three men were sailors – all crew members of the *AE2*, one of the first Australian submarines. The *AE2* was the first Allied vessel to penetrate the Turkish defences in the Narrows of the Dardanelles. To me, it's indescribably sad that these heroes of the Gallipoli campaign have lain here in Baghdad for the last 87 years, rarely visited and in a state of dusty, broken neglect. The Anzac Day service now firms as a long-overdue commemoration for the heroic sacrifice of these men and those who rest alongside them.

In the aftermath of our visit to the cemetery, I draft a plan to conduct a dawn service there on Anzac Day. The Americans are very enthusiastic about supporting the activity, to the extent that I almost feel a little guilty about how much effort they are prepared to expend. We plan to invite all the senior US military leaders as well as several of the ambassadors in Baghdad. This potentially high level of VIP attendance increases the risk immeasurably, so we plan for all possible contingencies; including attacks from small arms fire, rocket fire and suicide bombers. It'll be a slightly different Anzac Day dawn service to those we run back in Australia.

It becomes very apparent that this is going to be a significant military operation. A troop of armoured cavalry soldiers will form the outer perimeter in partnership with an Iraqi infantry battalion. Counterimprovised explosive device teams will sweep the roads all the way from our bases to the Baghdad War Cemetery. Explosive-detection-dog teams will search the car park and the area in the cemetery where the service will take place. Three sniper teams will position themselves on rooftops. A Predator drone will patrol overhead and provide a continuous picture of activity across the area. All of this is provided enthusiastically, in support of our event, and I am quietly overwhelmed by the response. The fallen Australians in that cemetery would have been proud.

Anzac Day, 25 April 2009, falls on a Saturday. On the Thursday prior, a suicide bomber attacks a group in the southern part of Rusafa in Baghdad city, a mere 8 kilometres from the Baghdad War Cemetery. There are conflicting reports of casualties, but the final toll appears to stand at 28 killed and 50 injured.

Just after midday on Thursday afternoon, another suicide bomber attack occurs in al-Muqdadiyah in Diyala province, north-east of Baghdad. The suicide bomber targets a restaurant and kills 47, injuring another 69.

On Friday morning, I brief Major General Swan on the security plan for the Anzac Day dawn service. I nervously seek his assessment of whether the residual risk is acceptable. I run through the threat assessment. The two bombings the previous day give us cause for concern. Is an Anzac Day dawn service worth the potential of having several VIPs killed? It's a tough decision.

Just after midday on Friday there is another big attack in Baghdad. A suicide bomber detonates his vest outside the Kadamiyah Shrine. The toll is frightening – a total of 53 people killed and over 110 injured. This double attack is only a few kilometres west of the Baghdad War Cemetery. The news of this attack breaks just as General Odierno is being briefed about the dawn service. In full realisation of the carnage that has just been inflicted, the Commanding General weighs up the risks and nods his concurrence to proceed.

In the early hours of Saturday, 25 April, everything begins moving. It's a clear night with no moon, but the lights of the city allow a grainy visibility. The US and Iraqi Army security perimeter around the Baghdad War Cemetery is slotted into place first. A team mounted in specialised vehicles that clear improvised explosive devices checks the roads through Baghdad leading to the cemetery.

In the Green Zone, we are up by 2.00 am and ready to move by 2.45. I jump into the back of one of the five Australian light armoured vehicles operated by the Embassy security detachment. In unison, my fellow soldiers and I don ballistic vest, anti-flash hood and gloves, helmet and goggles.

We arrive at the cemetery just as the explosive-detection-dog teams finish checking the car park. A few civilian vehicles and a truck sit around the car park, but the dogs confirm the absence of any traces of explosives. The sniper teams make their way up onto the rooftops. The Predator circles above.

By around 3.45 am, the Australian security detachment soldiers have set everything up in readiness for the service. They have manufactured flagpoles and national flags, and brought a lectern, a public-address system and a small generator to the cemetery. Tiny torches illuminate the white memorial stone and the flags. The light catches the sea of brown headstones around the central memorial stone – in the pre-dawn darkness, the effect is dramatic.

Young soldiers from the security detachment escort VIPs from their vehicles to an area next to the entrance archway. A convoy of American armoured trucks delivers all the Australian embeds and the other guests. After handing out programs for the dawn service and a host of candles, we call all the attendees forward to the memorial stone. There are over 100 people present.

We begin the dawn service at around 4.40 am when we mount a catafalque party. US Army Chaplain Dan Rice recites the invocation. The Australian Ambassador delivers a stirring introductory address. We join Chaplain Rice in singing 'O Valiant Hearts' with all the sincerity we can muster. Fittingly, the main address comes from the Australian National Commander, Major General Mark Kelly, delivered in a distinctly Australian twang that would have gladdened the hearts of the fallen Australians.

The VIPs are invited to lay wreaths at the memorial stone. The commander of the security detachment recites the Ode, and the bugler plays 'The Last Post'. The flags are lowered and we observe a minute's silence. As we stand amid the headstones with heads bowed, we can hear the Predator buzzing above us – I don't imagine many dawn services have been accompanied by such a tune before. It's a fascinating combination of one of the oldest Australian military campaigns with one of the newest.

The spell of silence is broken by the bugler's reveille. The flags of Australia, New Zealand, Britain, France and Turkey are raised to full mast. Dawn begins to creep over the horizon as the dark shadows fade. Brigadier Gould recites Ataturk's address, and our resident Kiwi intones the classic World War I poem 'In Flanders Fields'. Chaplain Rice closes the service with a benediction and we dismount the catafalque party. By now it is approaching 5.15 am, and there is enough light to spot the sniper teams on the surrounding rooftops. In closing, I thank everyone for coming and, on behalf of the Australian Ambassador, invite them back to the Australian Embassy for breakfast.

Few of the attendees have visited the cemetery before, and most will not have another chance, so they take the opportunity to have a quick walk around. The significance of the event is not lost on any of the participants. It may be some time before another Anzac Day dawn service is held at the Baghdad War Cemetery.

After 15 minutes, the personal security detachments begin to grow nervous and start herding their principals back towards the vehicles. The rest of us file back into the armoured trucks and follow. In the space of 30 minutes we've all left; all that remains are the wreaths on the memorial stone.

Given the feverish buzz of activity, I don't have a chance to meet up with Jasim, the caretaker. But Jasim finds one of my compatriots and hands him something for me. It's one of his prized Judo medals – a heartfelt 'thank you' for honouring his cemetery. It is a gesture that touches me to the core.

At the Australian Embassy, another team has been preparing a breakfast of barbequed steak, chicken and eggs. A rank of small Bundaberg rum bottles stands invitingly alongside the coffee urn. The Australians and Brits are happy to partake in a gunfire coffee, but the Americans are more reluctant. A couple of hours later, it is time to return to our bases, so we jump back into the armoured trucks for the run down Route Irish to Victory Base. It's been a good morning.

The Anzacs who fought for our freedom were a tremendously social breed and so, after a solemn dawn service to remember their sacrifice, we celebrate that night with an Anzac Day party at Aussie Island. We cater for 150 and about 300 turn up – we have clearly underestimated our popularity. I give a short impromptu speech about Anzac Day and what it means to us. Brigadier Gould takes the microphone to explain the Australian government's decision to end its contribution to the coalition. He also explains that we can't sing and we aren't very good at drill, but that we can throw a party.

We have asked the 56th Army Band to play for us, and they don't disappoint. They set up beside the empty pool and proceed to belt out great music for three sets. After the meal, the cigars come out. The near beer is a poor accompaniment. It's been a long day, but a very memorable one. Like those Australians in the Baghdad War Cemetery, I sleep soundly, knowing that this was an occasion of which I can be truly proud.

Taken Prisoner
at Fleurbaix

William Charles Barry, A Company,
29th Battalion, 8th Brigade AIF

William Barry was captured by the Germans in the battle of Fromelles on Wednesday 19 July 1916. He was one of more than more than 4,000 Australian POWs on the Western Front. Their story is little known.

The German artillery fire was growing fiercer every minute, in fact it was hellish and their shells were landing with great accuracy and killing the boys like flies. About 10 o'clock I shifted my position (and it proved a bad move for me) and was able to get into the German trench. No sooner was I there, when a shell struck the top of the parapet with a terrific explosion. Two boys standing alongside of me started to cry for their mother and I told them to cut that out, but pray to God to get them out of this hole. No sooner were the words out of my mouth, when another shell hit the parapet just above my head and I remember nothing more.

About daybreak I felt my legs being roughly pulled about and as I regained my senses, to my horror, I found myself surrounded by half a dozen Germans who were talking very loudly and seemed to be excited. My first thought was to speak to them, but my second one was to lay still and shammed dead, which proved in my case the better plan, for one of the enemy lifted up my leg and then let it go. I let it drop as though it was broken and without any more happening for the time, they all left me. My thoughts were now to try and get back and give the alarm that the enemy had retaken the trenches, but I must have become unconscious again, for I remembered nothing more till I woke up several hours afterwards and was able to move, although I was suffering pain.

Presently a number of the lads came along with their equipment and they informed me that Fritz had retaken the trenches during the night and we were all prisoners. About five minutes afterwards another party came along, under the charge of two Germans with fixed bayonets and they were treating the boys cruelly by bumping them with the butts of their rifles or prodding them with the bayonets. Just then two Germans came along and on seeing me laying on the ground, one came up and spoke in good English to me. The other was sighting his rifle and I fully expected to be shot, so I drew the German's (who turned out to be an officer) attention to him and he immediately ordered him away.

The officer, after looking at my clothing, informed me to my surprise that I was wounded and with a pair of scissors he cut the legs of my strides and showed me a gaping wound in the side of my right knee and another wound in the calf of the right leg. He then bandaged up the injuries using my field dressing then his own. When he had finished he started to ask for information. He knew what battalion, brigade and division I belonged to and was very anxious to know if our chaps would come back again, to which I replied that I hoped they would because I certainly would have a chance of getting back to our lines again. After trying to pump all sorts of information out of me, to which I answered with the most awful lies imaginable, he wanted to know how many Australians there were in France. I promptly answered between three and five millions and then the conscripts were to be called out. I cannot help laughing now when I think of the expression on his face as he exclaimed, 'Wass you a fria willie, a volunteer eh.' I said 'Yes.' You Australians are b***** cowards,' he roared. 'We are not at war with you, but you came over here last night and went hough,' (here he imitated a bayonet thrust). The German officer had lost all of his kindness to me know, so I asked him if I could see a doctor. 'No!' he roared. 'We have too many of our own wounded to look after.' Just as he left me he said something in German to a couple of soldiers standing nearby and I got one of the worst beltings that it was possible to give a man; in fact I was knocked unconscious for more than four hours.

When I came to my senses, I found myself in a dugout and I noticed that the buttons of my tunic were all undone and everything taken out of the pockets, including my pay book, wallet and money, nearly seven pounds in notes and cash. It dawned on me I had been fanned, an army expression for being robbed.

Eventually, without any more rough handling, I was handed over to two of the German Red Cross who carried me to their dugout and gave me a piece of their black bread (horrid tasting stuff it was) with a piece of bully beef and a drink of black coffee. The German who could speak English asked me if I felt cold. I told him 'Yes' and he brought me a German military coat. It was wet with blood, but that didn't matter. He also gave me a tin of bully beef and a piece more bread and left me propped up against a heap of earth.

It was the 21st of July and the sun was shining brightly and when I was left to myself for an hour, I was able to look around me and to my horror I was in a place where all the dead men were being stacked. I was sitting on the edge of a hole about 40 feet long, 20 feet wide and 15 feet deep and into this hole the dead were being thrown without any fuss or respect. Friend and foe being treated alike, it was pitiful to see the different expressions on their faces; some with a peaceful smile while others showed they had passed away in agony.

About midday, half a dozen of us wounded chaps were put on a horse ambulance wagon and were driven to a hospital a few miles away and were taken in and left waiting in a small room… The following day two Russian prisoners carried me on a stretcher to the operating theatre… On September 23rd a party of us were taken from this hospital and went to the railway station and were put on a Red Cross train. After travelling for three and a half days through Germany and along the valley of the Rhine, which by the way was beautiful, and we were kindly treated by the German staff on board. The train arrived at the town of Kempton, in the south of Bavaria.

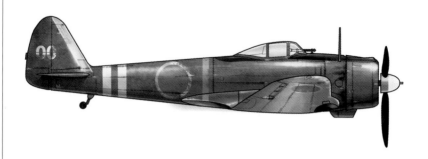

Low Flying Aircraft

You can have no idea just how hostile aircraft can be until they come to your area. Aircraft which bomb and strafe your position and wear a red circle should certainly be regarded with deep mistrust. In fact, the deeper the better. A six-foot-deep slit trench is an ideal place from which to mistrust them…

Corporal Brian Murray, 2 Sect 6 Topo Survey, New Guinea

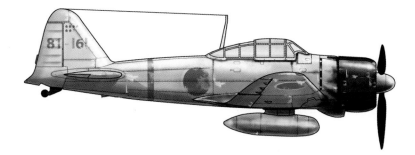

Letters From Timor

Chaplain Graeme Ramsden,
International Force in East Timor, 1999

I started my army service in Vietnam as a soldier with the Royal Australian Electrical and Mechanical Engineer Corps in 1968–69. In 1976, I was commissioned and served as a quartermaster, officer commanding a workshop and, as an instructor at the Land Warfare Centre.

In 1990, I undertook theological studies and was ordained as a deacon of the Roman Catholic Church and developed a wide pastoral experience with the church. In 1993, I commenced duties as a chaplain in the Australian Regular Army.

In 1999 I deployed on operations to support the Joint Support Unit with the international Force in East Timor (INTERFET). During the deployment, I was also appointed Deputy Senior Chaplain for the mission. I found that the operational deployment was a distinctive journey for each and every person that served with me. I wrote many letters home to share my experiences with my wife Dianne. These are just two of those letters – my first and last letters sent home to Dianne.

Wednesday 29 September 1999

Dearest Dianne,

It hasn't taken me long to discover that the local Timorese people are a wonderful people; full of spirit and genuinely appreciative of our being here. I love them dearly. Once they recognise that I am a padre, they call me 'Father' and they kiss my hand every time they see me. I could get used to that back home in Australia.

Water is a problem. We have to truck in jerricans and our drinking water is mainly 1.3-litre bottles imported from Australia. I had a shower last Sunday and hope to have another this Sunday, although I might treat myself to a shower on my birthday (1 October). What little electricity we have comes from small portable generators and is mainly for lighting. We will eventually get the larger KVA generators for power. I have found little use for money in Dili. Local labour is being encouraged and cleaning ladies will be hired and paid for on an individual basis. They will look after our rooms, called 'dongas,' and do our washing. In about a month, there will be a Frontline canteen operating selling all manner of comfort items for the troops. Postage to Australia is now free, even for parcels up to 20 kilos.

Please don't think I am threatened here. I am very confident we are over the worst and that we are no longer in danger. There is always a chance that someone may do something silly but the militia are just bullies and bullies don't take on the strong. The UN has passed a resolution on War Crimes and our assessment is that the TNI are busy getting all the 2 Early Days 14 bullies, the militia, and soldiers out of the country. We also believe if the militia was going to have a crack at us, they'd have done it by now.

I'm feeling good. I still feel a little queasy in the morning and am battling a rash in the private areas. The queasiness is, I think, from the Doxycyclin I take each morning to suppress malaria. Today I cut off my undies and threw them in the bin. I recall not wearing any in Vietnam and Singapore, so I'll do it here too. I was to find that the Americans call this form of dress 'free snaking'.

I have my appetite back, which is not good. It would be a crime if I was to put on weight in a country where people are starving to death. We are still on ration packs and will be for some time. I rather like ration packs and am in no hurry to move on. I feel well supported from home, not only by you, but also by the wider community.

All my love
Graeme.

Sunday 20 February 2000

Dear Dianne,

I have been here five months today and away from you five months and a day. But next Sunday I will be home again. On Sunday afternoon, we had a farewell from the children. It was down at the gym and there were about 1000 children there. When we first started to go up to visit the Sisters and the Children's Oratory on a Sunday afternoon, there were about 200 kids and they held it in the courtyard of the convent. Now they won't fit in there.

They had a program of singing and dancing for us. A group of young girls dressed in local costumes danced in bare feet. They came and got our doctor, Dennis Bartrum, General Cosgrove and me, and dragged us out the front. We had no rhythm and big boots and they had tiny little bare feet. They sang. Their poet recited a poem for us. The Sisters thanked us. The General spoke. The young people thanked us. The band played. They sang my favourite song. While it was going on, I leaned over to the General and said, 'A bloke should be able to have a cry now and then.' He nodded. When a little five-year-old girl came out in a nice pink dress and read a thank you note in good English, he leaned over to me and said, 'Now would be a good time.' Both of us were close to tears, it was very moving. Afterwards there was the usual hand-shaking, and kissing of the hand for me, and a hand out of a snack for oratory members.

All my love,
Graeme

You Don't Let Your Mates Down

By Craig Deayton

In memory of Private Reg Lawler 2/12th Infantry Battalion and
Private Allan Michael 'Mick' Deayton 7th Division AASC.

We moved into our first house in a not-so-wealthy suburb of Hobart in the spring
of 1990. Our neighbour popped his head over the fence on the day we moved in.
'Welcome to Lutana, son'. He asked my name and dropped his eyes to the ground
in thought at my answer. 'Not Mick Deayton's son!' he said. I nodded. It wasn't a
common name. 'Bloody hell, he was a mate! I was in the Middle East with your Dad!'
and at that Reg Lawler took off, limping down the driveway, back to his house to
rummage through his old photos. He came back ten minutes later with some small
black and white snaps of young diggers having a water fight at their camp in Syria.
I'd seen something similar in Dad's old photos but here was the complete story
of a long-ago afternoon's muck-up for several young men from the 7th Division's
Ammunition Supply Company, throwing water and sand over each other. Putting
Reg's and Dad's photos together, the incident now made some kind of mad sense –
who started it, who retaliated, who chased who past the bell tents.

Reg had more of the missing jigsaw pieces of my father's life to give me over
the next few months. They were great mates he said. Dad was 'one of the best'
according to Reg, 'a tough bastard, but straight as a die'. There were stories of his
life at war, stories he never told us, stories we never listened to. Unknown to us,
Reg was one of the silent old soldiers who came stiffly to attention around Dad's
grave in October of 1981 as the last post was played. They'd parted company in
1942 when Reg transferred to the 2/12th Infantry Battalion as the 7th Division

retuned from the Middle East to New Guinea. 'Bloody stupid move, that!' He'd wanted to be with his brother but wound up in the desperate fighting over the Owen Stanley Range. He'd been at Shaggy Ridge, where the Japanese fought to the last and rolled grenades down the near-vertical slopes as the Australians stormed the hill. He didn't want to talk about that. The bodies of the dead – ours and theirs – still bothered him, he said. He looked about him as if they lay around us at that moment.

Reg became the surrogate grandfather to our two small sons in place of the mate who had never known his own grandchildren. He and Madge kept an open house to our boys. 'He's coming over!' Madge would shout unseen over the fence when one of our toddlers disappeared next door – lured over by the open biscuit barrel and the luxuriant kindness of our old neighbours. Reg's handmade wooden toys were there at every birthday and Christmas.

One night things changed in our quiet street – sudden noises outside, angry shouting, scuffling. My wife was feeding our baby and she parted the curtains to look. A group of shadowy figures were gathered menacingly on the road, carrying iron bars. Two of them started smashing our picket fence, raining blow after blow. 'Come out, you *****!' they yelled; angry, violent threats. We thought we'd somehow provoked them by drawing open the curtain. We were not to know that their real target was hiding in our garden. He'd been running from them and chosen our overgrown front yard as a last refuge. The smashing and swearing continued, the fence disintegrating as we, cowering and frightened inside, phoned the police.

And then, as suddenly as it had come, it stopped. They drew off, iron bars aloft, walking slowly backwards, their free hands held up as if to ward off some unseen threat from the shadows. Away, up the road, they turned and ran. There was no reassuring police siren to drive them away, just darkness and quiet descending again while we watched through the darkened window and feared their return. A few minutes later the man they'd chased into our yard stood up from his hiding place and sprinted off in the opposite direction. It was over.

We lay awake till morning and when the light came, I went out to inspect the damage to our fence. Reg and Madge hadn't slept after that either and they came out to help me clean up the mess. 'Bloody wasters!' Reg said. He offered to help me build a new fence and he offered his theories on what had happened to society that this sort of thing should happen. 'Don't worry,' he grumbled, 'they wouldn't have wanted to set foot on your driveway.'

'You're a bloody silly old fool, Reg Lawler!' Madge spat out and proceeded to abuse him in highly colourful terms, cursing him roundly for his stupidity and recklessness in going outside during the turmoil.

Like the other half of that water fight in Syria, the other half of the story of that night slowly fell into place thanks to Madge. Woken by the commotion, swearing and smashing, and alarmed – as we were – that the mob were somehow targeting us, Reg had gone to his garden shed, taken his old 12 gauge shotgun from its case and slowly walked down the driveway with the weapon trained on the group. As he moved into sight under the streetlight, the sudden appearance of a figure in flannel dressing gown with a double barrelled shotgun trained on them brought a sudden and earnest rethink within the group, followed shortly after by a sudden and earnest running away.

Far from being stung by Madge's tirade, Reg was quietly proud of himself. 'Mick would have let "em have it' he grumbled under his breath, 'and so would I if they'd bloody set foot on the driveway!'

'Oh, you bloody well wouldn't have, you silly old bugger!' she said. Madge had had quite enough of stupid men to last a lifetime.

I thanked him, embarrassed that I'd been cowering inside while all this had been going on, despite Madge's urging me 'not to encourage him'.

I don't know if he would have fired the gun that night at all, let alone fired it at anyone. I don't even know if the gun was loaded.

But as he helped me pick up the pieces of our fence that morning, I did just quietly mention that perhaps Madge had a point and, grateful though I was, I didn't want to see him put himself at risk.

There was something in his eye and in the set of his jaw that recalled that young infantryman in those black and white photos as he answered me.

'You don't let your mates down, son'.

Nothing Worthwhile Doing Comes Without Sacrifice

Lieutenant James Fanning, DSM, 6th Battalion, the Royal Australian Regiment, Afghanistan, 2011

Our push into Deh Rawood is historic. This has always been known as the badlands — the 'Western Front' as it was always talked about. We are closer to British troops than we are to the rest of our battle group. We have Taliban Valley right on our doorstep and working with the Afghan National Army [ANA] is fantastic; it adds a whole new complexity to our operation. It gives us flexibility on how we engage with the locals and it has been a great experience for the boys to work with them. Instead of now just being Australian soldiers they are also for the ANA mentors. They set an example and teach them things that they would otherwise never learn and the Australian soldiers are very very good at that. We respond well to them and they respond well to us. Quite frankly that's the only way we will ever win this war because at the end of the day we are going home and they have to stay here. If we can get them to a point where they can be effective and give the locals a viable alternative to the intimidation that the Taliban provides then we have done our job.

Afghanistan is a staggering country, with a massive variety of cultures, environments and requirements of us as soldiers. The war here is local, although it's across the whole country for those people in front of our patrol base; they've concerned about what happens in their town. They live and die in that town, and for the vast majority of the thousands of small towns that fill the province and the country itself that's how they view the war — what's in it for them and their particular part.

There is no frontline as such but insurgents may control one town and another town is completely friendly to us, another town you can walk through the fields, along the footpaths and shake every hand that you come across. You can play with the kids and you feel safe and secure.

We have lost a lot of mates over here and I think a lot of the dealing with it will happen when we get home, when we have a big parade and everyone's together in a safe environment back at the barracks and able to talk about their experiences. Then we'll be able to talk about the boys who were lost, who didn't come back home… It will hit home when the guys are out at the bar with the usual crowd of mates and someone is missing – that's when it will hurt, really hurt.

It's a worthwhile job over here and as much as there is sacrifice nothing worthwhile doing comes without sacrifice.

The Agony of Killing

The author, a Vietnam veteran, wishes to remain anonymous due to the ongoing post traumatic stress suffered. His story has been verified and these are his words.

In early 1970 I led a 15-man patrol to the base of the Nuhi Tye Vhie mountains in Vietnam for a series of ambushes. These ambushes were to be conducted over a ten day period.

The second ambush we set I had an uneasy feeling and did not like the position so I placed my troops in an all-round defensive position and set out to recon a new site.

I briefed my men that I would go out via the machine gun position and return via the rifle group and that I would take at least an hour.

I took one man with me and left as planned, only to enter HELL and suffer till this day.

I found what I believed was a better ambush site. I was about to leave when the soldier with me indicated someone was coming down the narrow track.

I did not want to compromise our position or the position of my men I had left at the original ambush site so I signalled, by hand signs, to use bayonet only.

When the person was in my grasp I grabbed his legs and pulled him down and swiftly covered his mouth with my hand. My bayonet was at the base of his ribs.

He was moving uncontrollably all over my body, so with great force I pushed the bayonet up under his ribs until he moved no more.

After a good five minutes or more I knew nobody was behind him. This was the first time I looked at the PERSON that was bleeding all over me.

He was a boy no older than 15 years, caught up in a crazy war. I cried like never before. I still cry in my dreams to this very day.

The Bloke with the Pink Top

By James Hurst

It 'was a sad day' for employees of the markets when Pink Top's horse was auctioned. Perhaps his wife and children were there; perhaps it was the last place they wanted to be.

The fruit seller had achieved a lot before his life ended at Gallipoli. David John Simcock had moved to Perth from South Australia in the first decade of the twentieth century. He tried a number of ways to earn a living before investing in a fruit barrow to sell fruit in the city. Simcock's hair was 'pink – not red', and he was soon trading as 'The bloke with the Pink Top', or 'Pink Top'.

What really set Pink Top's business apart was his personality — he was a great spruiker. The stories about him are many and legendary. The *West Australian* newspaper stated at the time: 'His altogether novel methods of effecting rapid sales, his known wit and his no mean gift as an orator, made him a conspicuous figure and he soon became one of the identities of the city.' Pink Top became the 'object of much press attention as columnists, humourists, social writers and journalists chronicled his witty sayings and often spectacular doings.' The hard-working barrow vendor was soon doing well enough to establish a shop in the city. So popular did he become that crowds 'would gather to hear his spiel and read his witty signs.' On at least one occasion so many people stopped to listen that they blocked the tram-lines, and Pink Top was taken to court for causing an obstruction. In response he changed his signs in order to attract less of a crowd, inspiring him to quip: 'No more they'll plant their number nines, to block the tram, or steed. He's putting up some altered signs, that they who run may read.'

By 1914 things must have been going well for David Simcock. He now had a shop in Fremantle and was selling fish. He corresponded with the state premier, had married and been blessed with a daughter and son, aged 8 and 4 respectively, and had become a household name in Perth and Fremantle.

But then came the war. The 31-year-old father and businessman volunteered and became Private D.J. Simcock, 11th Infantry Battalion, the first battalion raised in Western Australia for the AIF. Hedley Howe later wrote that 'The highest tribute Australian soldiers ever paid to any of their comrades was "He is a good soldier".' Although 'clumsy and untidy in dress', Simcock soon earned that title. His 'doggerel about the Army and its officers', 'never failing sense of humour' and 'endless repertoire', ensured that he became well known and popular in camp.

Aboard the troopship carrying the battalion to Egypt were 2000 troops and one canteen. For a small commission, Pink Top took orders and money from the troops, queued up and collected and distributed the goods. 'He never made a mistake and no-one begrudged the commission he earned.' In fact, at Aden, with no shore leave granted, Simcock used his takings to buy crates of oranges from the boat-borne vendors and distributed them gratis to the troops.

During the men's training in Egypt, Simcock corresponded with the West Australian Premier Jack Scaddan, 'but what he had to say therein is certainly not for publication'. Like many others, Simcock took unofficial leave over the Christmas period, and, not for the first time, took the punishment metered out to him.

The 3rd Brigade were soon aboard troopships once more, being briefed for the impending operations at Gallipoli. At the end of one briefing, Lieutenant Mort Reid finished with the customary 'Any questions?' A pause followed, after which Pink Top requested an answer to an undocumented but 'still unsolved question about barmaids'. He was also concerned about submerged barbed wire. He put his mind to work and, 'sedulously encouraged by his mates', paraded before the colonel with his solution – 'a pair of leggings fashioned from a biscuit tin worn under the puttees. The colonel', it would seem 'was not impressed'.

Little is known about Pink Top's experience of what is probably Australia's best-known battle – the Gallipoli Landing. The unit history states that 'poor old Pink Top was killed early in the action through bobbing up and down in the trench, trying to get a look at what was going on. Unfortunately he bobbed up once too often.' The context of this account implies that this took place on 7 May, or nearly two weeks after the Landing. One newspaper account, written many years after Simcock's demise, stated that 'On May 2, 1915... while leading a charge against the Turks after his company commander had been killed', Pink Top 'had his head blown away by a piece of shrapnel...' A letter at the time stated that 'the officer in charge of his company was shot down and there being no-one to lead the men, Pink Top volunteered and took command. He gave the order to charge and they did not stop until poor Pink Top had just gained the top of the hill. Just as he said "Come on, boys" he was hit full in the face by shrapnel and blown to pieces.' Other stories also found their way home.

Only one eye-witness account of Simcock's movements on 25 April exists. Sergeant George Mason, Simcock's sergeant, recalled that Pink Top was detailed to remain on the beach to guard the men's packs, but he refused to be left behind and advanced inland with his platoon. This determination, to the point of turning a blind eye to orders, may ultimately have cost him his life. Mason and Reid accompanied a party that fought on the high ground of the left flank of the landing – the experience of their party, under Captain E.W. Tulloch, is well documented and a part of both history and folklore. Reid died there somewhere. Mason survived and that night was still fighting. Pink Top was with him. He ventured forward into the unknown to bring in a wounded man and did not return. There is a rumour that his unofficial tin leggings, visible beneath his tattered puttees, enabled his body to be identified a month later and buried. Many others who disappeared at the Landing have no known grave.

Ironically, on the day Pink Top probably met his end, the *Sunday Times* newspaper, wrote that they had received a postcard from Cairo of 'Pink Top drinking beer on the Pharoah's Sarcophagus'. After the war Pink Top's identity disc was recovered and sent to his wife.

In Perth's King's Park are many plaques commemorating the First World War's dead. One belongs to Lieutenant Charles Pope, the only member of the 11th Battalion to be awarded the Victoria Cross during the First World War. The award was posthumous. Alongside is the plaque to Private John 'Simpson', actually John Simpson Kirkpatrick, famous as 'the man with the donkey'. The next plaque bears the name of a private killed in his first day of war, fruiterer, father and volunteer of the first contingent, David John Simcock. His body lies on foreign soil among Australians and New Zealanders killed on 25 April after gaining the high ground that towers over the Anzac position. In Perth, his memorial plaque lies alongside those of a Victoria Cross recipient and national legend.

'Pink Top' is in good company.

Swing Low, Sweet Chariot

I was shot in the leg and was unable to continue back to my lines. As I lay in the snow with no feeling in my legs, I was picked up by a Chinese soldier and dropped in a trench, where I lost consciousness. I was then taken as a prisoner of war. The next day was 28 January, my 23rd birthday, and I was taken away to another building where I was given a spinal injection and a Chinese doctor, who spoke no English, performed an operation on my leg. As the Chinese doctor made the incision in my thigh, he explained to me in Chinese what he was doing. As I was lifted off the 'operating table', the stitching came undone and I thought I was in for another struggle when he again tried to close the wound. However, instead of trying to re-stitch me, he got an American field pack tin of sulphanilamide powder and sprinkled it all over the wound before I was carted off to another room. My spirit was pretty low at this time as no one spoke English, it was my birthday and I was in pain and alone. In the early hours of the following morning, when the pain was at its worst, a Chinese soldier cradled my head and sang, in perfect English, the Paul Robeson song 'Swing low, sweet chariot, coming for to carry me home'. This was a very moving experience that I will always remember. The soldier could not speak English to carry on a conversation, but I found out later that he had attended an American missionary school when he was a child. The next day, the pain in my legs had subsided and I started to regain my spirit. I felt like an exhibit at a zoo as I had a constant and steady stream of Chinese, both male and female, coming into the ward to have a look at the red-haired and blue-eyed prisoner.

Private Eric Donnelly, 3RAR, Korea

Training the Bodes

Terry Smith,
Australian Army Training Team,
Vietnam, 1972

When Australia withdrew the last of its combat forces and their logistics support group from South Vietnam on the 6 March 1972, it left behind a residual force. This force, called the Australian Army Advisory Group Vietnam (AAAGV), was made up of approximately 150 soldiers. It was in part established to demonstrate to the South Vietnamese and United States governments its continuing military commitment to South Vietnam. The Australian Army Training Team Vietnam (usually known by its initials, AATTV, or more simply, 'The Team'), of around 65 soldiers was the major unit under command of AAAGV. Although our role was little known, I was proud to be a member of 'The Team', training the Bodes, enabling them to continue the fight on their own.

Deployed in Phuoc Tuy Province, we were there to accomplish three main tasks:

- Assisting South Vietnamese instructors train junior officers and senior non commissioned officers of regular infantry units.

- Weapons, mine warfare and tactics training for the provincial Territorials.

- To help US Special Forces of the US Army Vietnam Individual Training Group (later renamed FANK Training Command) train Cambodian light infantry battalions at two training camps on Route 44 at the base of the Long Hai mountains.

Sixty-four members of 'The Team' served in FANK Training Command between 3 January and 29 November 1972. Stepping up to the role, this team helped train

27 light infantry battalions of the Cambodian Army numbering 13,600 across all ranks. Lieutenant Colonel (later Major General) Kenneth R. Bowra in his historical study of this program concluded:

> This operation is one of the least known, but most effective Foreign Internal Defence training assistance missions conducted by US Special Forces and can serve as a model for future Foreign Internal Defence missions in support of US policies and objectives… [It] is a classic example of using Special Forces as a force multiplier…

Although we had limited time and resources, the training regime was gruelling. Battalions followed the same intensive 12-week training course, irrespective of their standard of training or operational role. This was preceded by a three-week leadership course for 43 key officers and non commissioned officers of each battalion to prepare them to assist us instructors deliver the course.

Instruction followed the US Army model with a single instructor and his interpreter teaching a company of 150 or more Cambodians with perhaps one or two American or Cambodian assistant instructors. The use of live ammunition in tactical exercises was, by Australian standards at the time, quite high. Whilst this brought realism to training it was not for the faint hearted. In a letter I wrote to my wife I stated:

> Yesterday we put a battalion through a company attack exercise… the poor little buggers bunch up and fire their weapons every which way. They are terribly frightened of weapons and the only way to get them to move is to get out in front, which is not recommended for obvious reasons.

Nevertheless, despite the rawness of the majority of soldiers in each battalion, the rigidity of the program, and the limited time and instructors available to teach it, most of the Australians thought the content and training methods were about as good as they could be, given the US policy decision to train a light infantry force designed to combat guerrilla (rather than main force) units. This is best summed up by Lieutenant Colonel Jim Stewart, acting Commanding Officer of AATTV:

> In 12 weeks these motley assorted groups were trained to operate as a battalion, with organic support weapons and command and communications. Concurrently, unit and sub unit commanders were trained in command and control of unit and sub unit operations. Clearly, training and safety standards had to be compromised and any success the program achieved is attributable to the quality of the Team instructors and the relative enthusiasm of the

Cambodian officers and NCOs, who were dedicated and were now more capable of fighting the Khmer Rouge on their return to Cambodia.

Field training operations in a combat environment were a very important part of the training program. The final 12-day operation was the culmination of each battalion's training and enabled us to evaluate how well the battalion could put into practice the many lessons taught and its combat readiness.

The nature of these field operations, and their location, made it inevitable that FANK battalions would contact the enemy; however, we never deliberately let them walk into trouble. The Cambodians standard of training was not good enough for a stand up fight with communist main or regional force units. A report at the time highlighted one unit's actions during a contact:

> During contacts with the enemy the troops were disorganised and reluctant to fight, even to the point of running from the contact. Effective fire… never evolved. Machine gunners laid their weapons over the side of defilade positions and fired without looking at their target. They did not even use the bipods or tripods… Americans and Australians had to physically move troops into security positions…

The situation in Phuoc Tuy Province after the departure of the Australian Task Force quickly reverted to what it was before they entered it in 1966. A intelligence report from March 1972 noted:

> The rapid rundown of [allied] forces is providing a condition in which the [South Vietnamese] forces are unable to counter the re-establishment and strengthening of Viet Cong infrastructure and base areas throughout the province.

The South Vietnamese territorial forces were tied down defending population centres and trying to keep the major roads open. They rarely conducted mobile operations in depth against the enemy base areas which meant the enemy could go almost anywhere they liked, without challenge.

In April 1972 the North Vietnamese Easter Offensive burst into South Vietnam, Phuoc Tuy province. For three months it was the scene of heavy fighting and again in October, although at a much lower intensity. During this time 1600 enemy regular troops entered the province which brought the total number of enemy main forces in Phuoc Tuy, excluding the local guerrillas, to 3000. Units well known to the Australian Task Force; *33rd North Vietnamese Regiment, 274th Viet Cong Regiment, D445*

Viet Cong Battalion. 74th Viet Cong Artillery Battalion and local force guerrilla companies were all identified in action during April and May.

Twenty Cambodians were wounded in a mortar attack on the Long Hai Training Battalion camp on 6 April. Contacts, attacks by fire and a mine incident involving the 21st and 23rd FANK Battalions and the *33rd North Vietnamese Regiment* near Xuyen Moc occurred on 7, 12 and 13 April resulted in the deaths of four enemy and three Cambodians soldiers with 16 Cambodians and two US advisers wounded. Captain Adrian Roberts, who had fought in the Battle of Long Tan in 1966 summarised the situation in Phuoc Tuy in April 1972 as:

> It was for all the world to me as it had been in 1966, at the very beginning…
> as if we had never really been there…

The AATTV in 1972 were trainers rather than operational advisers. We were there strictly in a non-combat role. This meant we could accompany the Cambodians (and South Vietnamese) on their field operations but were not to attempt to initiate contacts with the enemy. There are, however, 44 contacts or hostile incidents involving the enemy and Cambodian battalions during our last several months of training. These resulted in the deaths of eight enemy soldiers, one wounded (escaped) and one captured. The Cambodians suffered 14 killed and 54 wounded, the Americans, two dead and eight wounded, and the Long Hai Training Battalion's (Vietnamese) recon platoon, six dead and eight wounded. Total allied losses were 22 killed in action and 70 wounded while training in Phuoc Tuy. My explanation of the situation was:

> It is true we are no longer in a combat role. …[but] we train in Charlie's back yard, so there are always contacts. This is not to be construed as a real war, however, because officially we are not on operations, but on field training exercises, just like back home. The only difference is the bad guys are real and nobody bothered to tell them about it not being fair dinkum, so they usually bowl a couple of Bodes over and shoot through.

The Cambodian battalions we trained were a mixed bag. Some were good, some bad and the others somewhere in between. It was easy to be critical of them but it needs to be remembered that up to 60% of their soldiers were straight from the villages or towns and, unlike the Australian infantry battalions, they were put into the field with just eight or ten weeks training. When later asked my own battalion I wrote:

You asked me how I felt about the battalion; proud. They never let me down once and would always give their best. They are such a childlike people it is a shame they are in a war. I wished I could have gone with them as they will have a way to go before they learn it all but perhaps we may have saved a few with our training here.

Roy Chamberlain served in FANK on his second tour of Vietnam. Thirty-five years after the end of the Vietnam War, Roy was back in Cambodia as a volunteer, helping clear land mines. When asked why he was doing this dangerous work he said:

...The second time I went back I helped to train Cambodian soldiers so they could go back to Cambodia and fight the Khmer Rouge. I felt we let them down. It was not a good feeling for the last Australian soldiers in Vietnam because we were leaving them...

He could have been speaking for us all.

Trimmed or Cut

Major General John Joseph Murray, DSO & Bar, MC, VD, Tobruk ,1941

In Tobruk was a member of the protective platoon that performed the function of guarding my HQ. He was known as 'Little Tich'. I cannot ever recollect him being referred to by any other title. Suffice to say, the name suited him to perfection. He was about five feet two inches in height and his small face was adorned with a huge, bristling moustache. On top of his soldierly duties, he was the HQ hairdresser. When I resorted to his tonsorial art we developed a short period of mutual understanding. In true barber's style he barraged me with questions: 'Nice day, Sir. Do you think Jerry will be over today? Will Turkey come in?' etc., and then he asked me how I'd like my hair cut. 'In silence,' was my reply. Silence reigned for a short time and then came a hushed tentative question, 'Would you like it cut or trimmed?' We were friends. I said, 'Why the odd question?' to which he replied, 'Well, Sir, the boys asked me to ask you that. They reckon that if you are getting it trimmed, we'll be getting out of here pretty soon, but if you want it cut, we'll be here for the duration.' I asked for a trim, not that I had any hopes at all in that direction, but one never knows. Besides, it helped my own morale.

A Scotsman always pays a debt

By Reg A. Watson

It was Anzac Day 35 years ago. I was having a beer in the local hotel when I struck up a conversation with an old timer from World War I.

We continued to guzzle the cold, clear liquid down our willing throats as our companionship grew. Although aging, Jock was a brawny Scot of immense physical stature who, it was obvious, could handle his drink as well as any man.

He had come to Tasmania as a boy, but had joined the Australian Army early in 1914 and had fought at Gallipoli. Jock was wearing an assortment of medals. I asked what they were for.

'Do you want to see another one, mate?' Jock asked.

'For sure,' I eagerly replied. The old Scotsman-turned-Digger pulled from his hip pocket a small black box which he placed on the bar between us away from the eyes of others. He opened the box and pulled out the contents, which he held temptingly before my eyes.

I looked and looked a second time as I wanted to be sure. 'Blimey!' I exclaimed. 'A German Iron Cross! I suppose you found it? Got it off a dead German perhaps?'

'Nay cobber,' he answered in his mingled Scottish-Australian. 'I won it.'

'But heavens, Jock, this is a German decoration. How could you win it from the enemy?'

'There came a point in the war, just a small point, a moment in time, when they ceased to be my enemy. I realised that they were men like us.'

'But…' I began again, '…how could you win it?'

'I won it,' he persisted.

There was a silence. He put his mug on the counter and looked straight ahead as though time had ceased.

'Do you want to hear how I did?' turning to me and asking. All I could do was nod. He began his remarkable and true tale.

'After the hell and failure, but bravery of Gallipoli, the Australian troops were transferred to Europe. They were reorganised and I became a part of the 2nd Division of the 1st Anzac Corps and was sent to form a part of General Gough's Fifth Army,' he said.

And what waited them was the stinking cesspool of carnage and horror of the First Battle of the Somme.

Adolf Hitler fought in this battle that was waged between those remarkably brave Germans and their equally brave enemies, the British, French and Commonwealth troops. The price of glory was to be high.

Jock's corps was moved up the front on 19 July 1916. They attacked south towards the French town of Fromelles. It was an ill-planned attack and although the Australians fought bravely the casualties were more than 5,500.

The Germans hearvies pounded the corpses and the battlefield became an open cemetery. Then one day German horsemen surprised Jock and 30 other Australians while recovering dead and wounded.

Jock was in the front row, kneeling with fixed bayonet. They came like God's Wrath. One horse cleared Jock's bayonet and the rider, an officer, leaned to slash him with his sword.

Jock met him eye to eye and for some unknown reason, the officer changed his mind. Was there a flicker of humanity in his eyes? Whatever the reason, he struck with the flat of his sword.

When he came to Jock was among the dead. All his comrades were dead or wounded, but Jock's life had been spared.

I thought this was the end of Jock's narrative, as he stopped talking. 'But how did you win the medal?' I asked again.

'Just hold ya horses, mate. I haven't finished,' he responded.

The savagery of the war was maintained and a year later found our Jock amazingly still alive. In September 1917, the 1st Anzac Corps formed the spearhead of the next thrust against the ridge east of Ypres.

Trench warfare was the order of the day. The degrading spectacle that Jock knew at the Somme and elsewhere was repeated at Ypres.

Jock and his companions lay in a trench on the border of non man's land.

He had long since grown accustomed to filth, misery and death. Most of his mates were dead or had been sent back terribly wounded; he had outlived them all. He grew into believing that providence was on his side – why? He could not answer, but how else could he have survived? Jock thought he heard a groan. Yes, it was a groan not far away – just in the next ditch. His cobber heard it too. There was no mistake – someone was alive out there. 'Come on, mate,' he said motioning to his friend, 'Let's creep over and bring him back.'

On elbows and knees they crawled over the top and long the edge with a nerve-racking slowness. They had reached the ditch and slid into it.

The mud that lay on the bottom of the ditch had turned into a consistency of sticky butter. The two Australians ploughed their way to the wounded man.

'By God, he's a Hun!' yelled the other. Jock looked squarely at the enemy. It was a young German officer who had taken a machine-gun bullet in the breast. He was in terrible pain.

The German muttered, gasping for breath, 'I beg you, Englander, kill me. I beg you; put an end to my pain.'

Jock's companion drew his bayonet, but Jock restrained him.

'No,' he said. 'Let him be!' All too clearly Jock's mind recalled the other German officer who had spared his life. One good deed demanded another, a life for a life.

Jock held the water can to the man's mouth and slowly and with difficulty he began to drink. The cool water revitalised the wounded man.

'Thank you,' he croaked.

'I'll take ye back,' Jock simply said.

'But Jock,' his mate protested, 'He's the enemy. Besides you'll both be killed.'

'I'll be takin' him back!' he repeated. 'I've' a debt to pay.'

He heaved the man on to his shoulders and started. First he trudged, maintaining his balance with difficulty, up the walls of the ditch, then onward to the enemy's fortifications. It wasn't far, but it was a way of possible death.

Strangely, oddly, nobody fired on him. Not a shot.

Incredulous eyes gazing across no man's land watched Jock's journey. In those few moments English, French, Australian and German were united in peace.

Jock stood there looking down into the enemy's trench. Two Germans jumped from their hole and helped the man from his shoulders.

Jock knew his debt was paid and turned to leave.

'Wait!' a voice called.

Another German officer speaking good English said simply, 'Thank you.' Jock saluted. 'What is your name?' The German captain asked. 'And your address?'

'I am not going to ask what division,' he added. 'That would be unfair.'

'And?' I asked.

'I told him,' Jock said.

'And what happened then?'

'That night I managed to crawl back okay; they wouldn't let me go before dark. I reported what I had done.' I let him continue, not interrupting.

'I was warned that I could expect trouble for what I had done. After all, he was the enemy.

'But nothin' was done; we all had other things to think of. Then the war ended and we came home and I came back to Hobart. Sometimes I thought of the German officer, wondered if he was alive, but never expected to hear more of it.

'One day I was called to headquarters. "Was I so and so?" asked the commanding officer.'

'That's right,' I replied.

'Here's something from the enemy – a present.' And he handed me this.

I looked at the cross once again, lying on the bar. Without another word Jock picked it up and placed it back into the black box.

'Surely something to be treasured,' I said.

'I do – it's my hope for a better world.'

That was the first and last time I saw Jock. For many years I looked for this Scotsman on subsequent Anzac Days, who believed in paying a debt, but I was never successful.

They Are Just Like You

The dead must be brought back to the section position, now in all-round defence. You never know when the enemy may counter-attack. You drag the dead enemy by their feet. This is easier than carrying them. You grasp the end of their trousers. They feel damp and they are slippery because of the blood. As you drag a body into the section position, the shirt gets pulled up around the neck, exposing the bloodied torso; it is not a pretty sight. The arms are stretched up behind the head. The bodies are bent and broken from battle. They are still sweaty, and stained with blood. You gaze at the enemy soldier. His life is spent. It is then you realise that he was just like you. He was doing his job for his country. But it cost him his life.

Private Ian Cavanough, 2RAR/NZ (ANZAC), Vietnam

A Soldier's Flower

Corporal William O'Neill, Royal Australian Electrical and Mechanical Engineers

As a young army recruit, it did not take long to realise that my life had been changed and might never be the same again. Not only was I issued with a uniform and equipment, I had also been inducted into a platoon of men who were all to become my brothers for better or worse.

There I was with a new way of life and a new family with whom I would be living in a hut of wartime vintage.

Over the years I lived in a series of these abodes which consisted of every thing from huts, tents, marquees and even a hole in the ground. But, despite their Spartan appearance, they became our retreat from the regimentation of army life.

There were many things that could be done to soften the strict Infantryman's layout. A pin-up here and there, a civvy shirt reserved for leave or a stack of letters from a loved one tied with a ribbon.

The hut itself was well maintained, with fire buckets and extinguishers hung by the door. Brass plates polished so well that the instructions were illegible. Floor boards were scrubbed white. Beds were aligned as if it were they that were on parade.

The exterior was kept in pristine condition; windows polished, never a cigarette butt to be found and wooden stairs worn smooth with the tramp of many boots. Around those stairs was an arrangement of stones, whitewashed and proudly displaying the name of the relevant platoon.

But there was one other important addition that was found at either side of those stairs. In every camp with out exception, there grew a humble geranium. The colours were never the same and of little importance. It was the plant that mattered, for it had a special message that I was later to learn.

These plants must have been from very hardy stock for some had grown there through many generations of my brother soldiers, and had been subjected to every indignity that it was possible to endure.

One hot day I sat on a set of those stairs with an old mate who would be more correctly referred to as 'an old sweat'. I noticed he had gone to the trouble of walking to a near by shower block with a bucket and wending his way back again just to water these geraniums. When his labour was finished, and he once again sat by my side rolling a smoke, I asked him why he went to such trouble on such a hot day. He explained that, as a young Digger on the outbreak of war, he had first seen these geraniums growing by the doors of huts around the camp. He had asked why they were there and was told by the old hands that they served two purposes. A soldier returning from leave would often try to take a little bit of home with him. So he would scrounge a piece of some plant that would remind him of his loved ones. Many plants did not survive the harsh life but the humble yet hardy geranium did.

As well as providing lonely diggers with a memento of home, it was believed that geraniums prevented snakes from crossing the threshold where they were planted. Perhaps that is why they are listed on the cargo manifest of our First Fleet.

As a young soldier I travelled to many more camps and made my home in many more huts, but I always thought back on that old digger's story when I noticed a geranium by the door of these huts.

Over the years I have spent some time revisiting the army camps that I once lived in, and have always come away with at least one geranium. Now when spring comes and the ache of old age leaves my bones, I like to wander through my garden. As I pass each geranium I 'scrounged', I name them from my former homes of long ago. Ingleburn is red, there is a white from Kapooka, an almost black from Puckapunyal. There are some from Greta, Broady, Singleton, Bandiana, Silver City…

Too many camps and too many geraniums to name, but I often think of that old Digger who sat with me that day and told me the story of 'The soldier's flower'.

So if you are lucky enough to live near a camp or where one has been, keep an eye out for a struggling geranium that some young soldier brought from home.

Moya Moya – Beersheba

Henry Gullet, Official Historian, Palestine, 1917

The Battle of Beersheba took place on 31 October 1917, as part of the Sinai and Palestine campaign during World War I. This was the scene of the charge of the Australian 4th Light Horse Brigade. They covered nearly 6 kilometres to overrun and capture the last remaining Ottoman trenches, and secure the surviving wells at Beersheba.

The night brought no rest for the light horsemen. Circumstances necessitated a strong and alert outpost line, and every man who could be spared was put to work to water the horses. Except for the drink on the previous night near the Wady Hesi, the animals had not been refreshed since leaving Beersheba, and the brigade was threatened with crippling losses. All the little villages on the flanks and rear were exploited for water, but the wells were from 100 to 250 feet deep. With the exception of an occasional antiquated water-wheel, the only appliance for raising the water was a bucket and a rope, and most of the ropes had been removed by the natives.

To water 2,000 thirst-stricken horses was, under these conditions, a task exceedingly laborious and slow. All night the crooked little streets of the mud-built, straw-thatched villages were packed with restless, thirsty horses, and gaunt, dusty, unshaven men, careless of their exhaustion in their desire to relieve their animals, and in the buoyancy of the indescribable sense of sweeping victory. Where ropes were missing they were replaced with bridle-reins and telephone wire, and cattle and horses, thus attached to the buckets and walking out in a straight line, hauled the water from depths as great as 200 feet.

Mingled with the troops and their horses were crowds of dirty, ragged, picturesque natives, who had been denied their supply during the fight and now, very thirsty, were clamorously fighting for their share. Telephone wire saved the brigade. All night, and until late on the following day, the water was raised bucket by bucket, and the work went on until all the parched horses had been relieved. In the areas where prisoners were assembled the horror of war was seen at its worst. Hundreds of hapless Turks, fighters for a cause for which they knew no enthusiasm and which was even beyond the understanding of men so simple and ignorant, moaned and cried in their sickness and thirst. 'Moya! Moya!' (water! water!) sounded all through that hideous night; and the light horsemen, deeply moved by pity for a foe whom they always regarded with respect and even kindliness, shared their own scanty supply with the afflicted prisoners, and worked the night through to bring them a little ease.

The Landing:
First Clash with Turks

William Cridland, 1st Field Company Engineers, AIF, 1915

All troops were assembled at Lemnos, the advanced base, and on the evening of 24 April 1915, the assaulting units were taken on board transports and warships to the Gulf of Saros. On arrival they were transhipped on to barges to be taken inshore.

A and B Company of the 9th, 10th, and 11th Battalions were chosen as a covering party, and 20 sappers, non-commissioned officers and an officer each from Nos. 1, 2 and 3 sections of the 1st Field Company. Engineers were chosen to go in as a demolition party with the covering party. I had the honour of being one of the chosen of No.1 section, and we had to go in with A and B company of the 9th Battalion. My section and the 9th Battalion were very fortunate in that we went from Lemnos to the hopping off place on the HMS *Queen*, the flagship of the Mediterranean Fleet. All ranks aboard treated us with the usual British naval hospitality, and we were all able to get a decent sleep in bunks, and on waking, a hot bath and a jolly good feed. Then, to cap it all, the canteen was thrown open to us, and the sailors packed us with their issue of chocolate.

In the early hours of the morning came the clear but low order to fall in. All lights were out, and the night was pitch black. Each man's load was evened up as well as could be, so I'll mention what I had – the usual full marching order, not forgetting rifle and bayonet, 250 rounds (the dinkum stuff too), emergency rations, pick, shovel, wire cutters, one dozen sand bags, and a case of gun cotton. How we managed to go down the rope ladders into the barges, then through the water and up the sand beach, God alone knows, for I don't as each barge had its full complement.

At last all barges were ready, and we were taken in tow by steam pinnaces. The moon had disappeared prior to our leaving the ship, but, looking back, we could see the black forms of the battleship following in our wake ready to cover our attack. Here we were at last launching out into the unknown, but it was a long-looked for event, after over eight months' hard, rigorous training at home, on board ships, in Egypt, and at Lemnos. However, our thoughts were suddenly checked by the report of a solitary rifle shot away up in the hills.

Every man realised that the supreme moment had arrived, and presently, Hell was let loose, but so far there was only one side having a go. Full speed ahead raced the pinnace towing the barges, then, swinging clear, left us travelling inshore. Now, the little middies, standing erect, grim, determined and heroic, directed the barges, swinging them clear of one another.

Lieutenant Mather, realising that the barges afforded no protection from the murderous rain of lead from rifles, machine guns, and artillery, told us to go overboard and make for the beach. His advice was promptly followed. We were, of necessity, compelled to gain what cover was offering, in order to take a spell, for, after struggling through about 40 yards of water and then up the beach with our load, we were somewhat blown. This, as near as I can remember, was in the vicinity of 4.20 am. After a very short breather Colonel Lee reminded us of the job on hand. Now was our turn, and, with fixed bayonets, we started off up the hill, dragging ourselves up with the assistance of the undergrowth in places. Eventually we gained the top, and I think all our casualties there were caused by snipers and shrapnel. There were about seven of us in a group, and we decided to move with caution, for some of our own cobbers coming up behind could very easily take us for Turks, for we were more like ragged tramps than anything else.

Our decision proved a blessing, not only to ourselves, but to those coming up. For, lying hidden as we were, we began picking off the Turks – some at very close range, too. As our numbers increased, we began to move forward till a messenger came up with an order that all engineers had to report back and commence the establishment of a line of defence, and cut steps up the cliff so that travelling would be made easier. It is difficult to remember the position of the job I had to carry out, that of cutting steps in the hill. But, as near as I can judge, it was that steep portion leading to Russell Top. Whilst engaged on this task, General Birdwood stood talking to me for a while, and was nearly sniped. Later he informed me that it was an occasion he would never forget.

From this job I went up the hill to assist in some trench running, and as soon as I got there a sniper got busy from across the gully; but he did not reign long, as one of our chaps sent him to Allah. That evening my section had a job of trench running somewhere up Shrapnel Gully. Considering the incessant blaze of rifle and machine gun fire all night, it was a wonder that any of us were left.

When one considers the geographical formation of the country, it is amazing to think that we ever got a footing on the Peninsula at all.

Hells Orchestra, Polygon Wood

Captain Alexander Ellis,
29th Battalion, AIF, Belgium, 1917

Our artillery opened in a single magnificent crash and thousands of shells screamed through the air and burst in a long, straight line of flame and destruction about 200 yards ahead of the waiting infantry… the 4,000 men of the six attacking battalions dashed forward at a run. Somewhere behind the line of destruction lay their victims, shuddering in their pill boxes, staggered by the sudden commotion, dazed by the concussion of the shells… then, slowly, very slowly it [the artillery barrage] crept forward. A long line of skirmishers disengaged itself from the dense mass of men and followed the advancing screen of shells… Above their heads thousands of machine gun bullets cut the air as they whistled shrilly past on their destined way, and the strident din of many Vickers guns throbbed through the troubled morning air. But these were but the tinkling woodwind notes in the hell's orchestra that played about them. For the deafening crash of the rapid firing 18-pounders, the hoarser roar of the scores of heavy guns behind them and the stupefying concussion of shrapnel and high explosive shells in the barrage in front were by now all mingled in the hideous rhythmical clamour of the perfect drum–fire barrage. Thus, at 5.50 am, on 26 September 1917, the Division [5th Division] launched into the Battle of Polygon Wood.

Lucky Miss from an IED

Corporal Adam Marsh, 6th Battalion, the Royal Australian Regiment, Afghanistan, 2011

We found a wooden no metal content pressure plate [part of an Improvised Explosive Device - IED] on the road the first one in province that was placed there for us when we were pushing east. Luckily for us we put a hide in a little bit before that. The engineers went down there and had a look, the dog got a hit and had a bit of a reaction to it. The engineers said they would go suss it out. They could'nt find anything and were walking back when one of them said, this doesn't feel right and he went back and had another look and they found a 20kg palm oil container with a wooden stake no metal content pressure plate. We blew that in place.

That day we got shot at as well, the whole platoon crossing open ground. The Taliban will just wait all day as they know we are going to withdrawal, they just waited, chose their ground well and arced us up when we were in the open, the boys spread, everyone running for cover - it was all right - the choppers came and could break contact.

Water and Garbage Run at Nui Dat

Corporal Dave Morgan, 104 Signals Squadron, Vietnam

I will never forget my very last work party. I was rostered on to do the water and garbage run (in a Land-rover and trailer) around the 104 Sigs lines. Part of the run included the wet garbage scraps from the kitchen. These were all bound for the Nui Dat garbage tip.

One of my shift workers, a 'Nasho' (National Serviceman), Sig Graeme Stevens, is rostered on with me. Stevo as we all call him was a likeable bloke, a farmer from Gawler in South Australia. However, with Stevo you could never tell whether he was serious or joking, as he had a perpetual smirk on his face.

Stevo didn't like the army and was pretty pissed off when he got called up for National Service. Forever grumbling about the army and the government, he proclaimed it would have been better for him to remain a farmer and grow food for the country.

We picked up the last rubbish bin which was next to an open roof shelter, a waiting area for passengers about to board choppers. Waiting in the shelter were several high ranking Australian and US Army officers in clean neatly pressed uniforms with spit polished boots. We must have looked a scruffy mess in our dripping wet, dirty, sweaty greens.

> 'Look at these f****** big brass bastards in their clean uniforms,' mutters Stevo as we lift the heavy drum full of rubbish to the back of the trailer. 'They wouldn't know how to get their hands dirty. Doesn't that just give you the shits, Morg?'

We got into the Land Rover and Stevo put his foot down. There's a screeching of tires and the last two drums on the trailer tumble off onto the bitumen. The wet kitchen scraps splatter in all directions; unfortunately this included the direction of the officers and onto their shiny boots and the lower parts of their uniform. Stevo slammed on the break and I looked back and see a pretty pissed off group of officers.

'Idiots!' they yell. 'Where's your brains and what kind of soldiers are you?'

Then one of the officers walks up to the driver's door.

'And get that smirk of your face, Private, or I will charge you,' he yells, inches from Stevo's face.

'What's your unit, Corporal,' another yells. 'Get this mess cleaned up straight away.'

Thankfully the chopper arrives just after this event and the chopper's crew signal for the waiting passengers to get aboard. We watch the six angry officers trudge despondently through the wet slush to the chopper. It takes us half an hour to clean up the mess, shovelling the muck into the bin, accompanied by thousands of flies. Our arses were saved thanks to that chopper arriving when it did.

A Medic in the Battle of Lone Pine

Private Edward Joseph Smalley, 3rd Battalion, AIF, Lone Pine, 1915

One of the most striking personalities to fall in the attack at Lone Pine was Private Smalley, a stretcher-bearer, the 'Gunga Din' of the battalion. Colonel Burnett wrote of this soldier in the history of the 3rd Battalion AIF:

He was unassuming – a square-faced, determined – looking chap, practically unknown outside his own company during those strenuous months at Mena. He worked for weeks on the Peninsula as no human being worked before. The cry of a wounded man would bring Smalley to his side. His strength and energy were superhuman. Everyone knew him. Everyone admired and wondered at him. I saw him on many occasions going round quickly cleaning the rifles of the men who were sleeping after coming off post.

'What about sleep yourself, Smalley?' I used to ask him, but his only reply was, 'I'm all right, sir, these poor fellows are tired.' I remember him before the charge at Lone Pine, covered all over with field dressings, 'to fix up some of the poor chaps', as he put it. He was hit in the stomach going over, and died almost immediately, saying only, 'Leave me, leave me, I'm done.' And so passed one of the most self-sacrificing, noble and courageous men who ever wore the Australian uniform.

NX15705 Cpl. J.H. EDMONDSON.
K.I.A. 14-4-41. VC 2/17 BN.
AIF.

The Tobruk Standard

Major General John Joseph Murray, DSO & Bar, MC, VD, Tobruk ,1941

A Broadcast address made by Major General Murray circa June 1941 to Australian soldiers via a world shortwave link-up.

Here in Tobruk we've just learnt that the Commonwealth Government is raising another war loan. This time it's for a hundred million pounds. That's a lot of money, but we've got to find it somehow. We're fighting an enemy who has staked everything on this war and who's forcing his own people and those he's conquered to make severe sacrifices in the hope of victory. We don't think for a moment that he will win. For six months in Tobruk we have been fighting the Germans and Italians and we know they're not good enough to win, provided our men have anything like a fair chance. But before we are sure of winning, we must make the same sacrifices as the enemy has made. Nothing short of complete national effort can bring us victory. Half-measures are no good, and the sooner we stop thinking that they are, the better. As Australians we're inclined to be satisfied with 'that'll do' or 'that's good enough' – but that standard won't do. Nothing will do short of what has been called the 'Tobruk Standard'.

I think I can talk about the 'Tobruk Standard' because I have the honour to command the infantry brigade which has been longest in Libya. The men under my command have helped to set the 'Tobruk Standard', and I'd like to tell you the kind of standard they've set.

They've been courageous and self-sacrificing – they wouldn't be good Australians or good Britishers if they hadn't been. But they've set a standard of cool courage that kindles memories of the Anzacs. Take this case: one Easter Monday the Germans attacked us with all their power. They were repulsed. You probably know the story of that repulse. But even so, it's worth repeating two things. During the night, about fifty Germans were met in no man's land by an officer, a corporal and five men. Our small party, without hesitation, charged with the bayonet, killing many Germans and compelling the remainder to retire in disorder. It was one of the most gallant things I've seen or heard in two wars. The corporal was Jack Edmondson. He was awarded the VC. Later, when the German tanks penetrated our line or perimeter posts, the infantry held their ground and, by so doing, they were able to beat off the German infantry attack which followed the tank attack. No infantry had ever done this before, and the Germans couldn't understand the courage of men who kept on fighting after their posts had been overrun by tanks. This sticking power, this refusal to give way, no matter how black the outlook – this has saved Tobruk.

Then they've shown another kind of courage – the daring, almost brazen initiative which had led parties of half a dozen or so to storm enemy strongposts or engage enemy patrols. Here is a case: some two miles outside our defences there was an Italian strongpost held by about fifty men. They had a number of machine-guns and anti-tank guns and were protected by mines, barbed wire and booby traps. An officer and ten men raided this post and killed at least fifteen and wounded many more. They crawled through the wire and the booby traps and they charged the post from the rear. One sergeant, a slight lad of twenty-one, killed or wounded at least five Italians himself, and even in the heat of the struggle had the presence of mind to stop and search his victims for tell-tale papers. The patrol leader was wounded as he went in, but that didn't stop him. He was determined to get a prisoner and, at one stage, he had two Italians by the scruffs of their necks trying to drag them from a trench. He only let them go when a hand grenade burst right in front of him and wounded him again. But he led his patrol back and sang as he came in.

I could talk for hours about instances like this one, but the men of Tobruk have needed more than courage. They've needed that optimism for which Australians are famed. In the early days here they saw our airmen shot out of the sky, overwhelmed by sheer numbers. Then they were dive-bombed almost with impunity and they couldn't hit back. They've seen enemy tanks in fifties and sixties and our own tanks in fives and sixes. They've been at the receiving end when heavy German mortars have been in action and they've had nothing to answer with. But what did they do? Did they throw in the towel? Did they say, 'We can't carry on in conditions like these. We must have this and that before we will fight?' Certainly not. They just gritted their teeth and defied the enemy with what equipment they had. The Germans scattered leaflets appealing to the troops to surrender after the disasters of Greece and Crete. Our troops' reply was to nail one of the leaflets to the mast in the main square of Tobruk and to put with it a banner marked, 'Come and get it'. That's the 'Tobruk Standard'.

But they needed more than courage and optimism. They've needed patience and plenty of it. For four months now they've been holding on without much activity. They've had to put up with heat, dust, salty water and not very varied food. They've done their share of grumbling at times, but they've even done their grumbling with a smile. They've never let discomforts or hardships get them down, they've only grown more keen to have a crack at the enemy which has made them fight in such Godforsaken country. But the waiting has tried their patience, especially in the salient. Conditions there have been anything but easy. Yet they've not only held their ground, they've forced the enemy back hundreds of yards and then dug themselves in again in new, improvised positions. To relieve the boredom of waiting, they've worked hard to make their positions better. Even during their spells in reserve, they've worked on new positions, drilling, blasting and digging their way through the unfriendly rock from early morning till dark, in heat and sandstorm. And by doing this they've made Tobruk infinitely stronger than it was when they came here.

Those are some of the elements of the 'Tobruk Standard' — courage, initiative, optimism, patience, ceaseless toil and, if necessary, complete sacrifice. This is the only standard which will win this war, and in it you won't find any room for complacency. You won't find it in Tobruk, because you can't live in a fortress with an enemy at your gate and still be complacent or still think that half-measures will do.

We know that we will win only if everyone does all he can and gives all he can. I think from what I've said you'll realise that the Tobruk men have made a standard and they've kept to it. They've shown that they are worthy of the total backing of every Australian. The kind of backing they need is the backing of guns and tanks and planes and the backing of the money that will buy these things. Without that, the war is going to be more costly in human lives and longer in the winning. But if we get the equipment and the money that is urgently needed, we can go right on from here to victory.

Operation Buffalo

Eddie Wright, 3rd Battalion,
the Royal Australian Regiment, Korea

I was the platoon signaller with 6 Platoon B Company on 13–14 August 1952. We were the assault platoon in Operation Buffalo. Lieutenant George, Sergeant Frewin and I were platoon Headquarters (HQ). I was to keep contact with our company HQ and had some fire tasks with the Centurion tanks and mortars. Also, I was to take over the flame thrower if Sergeant Frewin became a casualty. So I was well and truly loaded up with a few tasks if things went drastically wrong.

We crossed the Sami-Chon valley through the burnt-out village of Song-gok to our forming-up area at the bottom of the hill to assault. When Zero Hour arrived, we commenced our assault with two sections forward, HQ in the centre, and one section behind.

We ran into problems right from the start, as the Chinese had a listening post with two men manning it. The lead section on platoon HQ's right dispatched the two Chinamen to the land of their ancestors.

We jumped over the first lot of trenches and our artillery started to land onto the objective to our front. We continued the assault. Platoon HQ had lost the flame thrower, but we continued the assault anyway.

Lieutenant George yelled that without the flame thrower we were going to have a hard time trying to get the Chinese out of their underground bunkers. It was then that I saw that he was on fire from phosphorous. We were assaulting at a fair pace, and I chased after him and managed to tackle him with a good rugby tackle and started to throw dirt all over him trying to put out the flames, and he was calling me all the names that he could think of. I don't think he realised what I was trying to do.

It didn't take more than a few seconds to get the flames out and brush the phosphorous off and he then got straight up. He didn't bother to say thanks, and was off to catch up with the lead sections, leaving me to catch up with him. This is when things started to get a bit hairy for me.

There were artillery and mortars and tanks firing from our side, and now the Chinese mortars started to get stuck into us. At this time I could no longer see the platoon commander, so I continued to move to the top of the hill. I couldn't find him or any of the platoon. I then went into this small saddle and came across a few dead Chinese and wounded. I decided I wasn't in a very welcoming place so I moved towards our lines off the saddle.

As I staggered off, I fell into a very deep Chinese trench. As I picked myself up, I was just in time to see a group of Chinese coming out of a large bunker. I had only one magazine left, so I pressed the trigger and let them have the whole magazine, and started to run along the deep trench. I hoped to God that the Centurion tanks had collapsed the trench somewhere along the way. My prayers were answered. They had done a good job and I was able to get out and continue down the hill.

Nearing the bottom, I came across one of our wounded. I helped him up; he was in a terrible state. Phosphorous was burning into his scalp and both legs. I got him

down to the paddy field and took off my flak jacket, and then my shirt. I doused my shirt in the paddy field muck, ripped it into pieces, and wrapped it around his head and legs, and it calmed him down a bit. We continued along the valley floor until our faithful stretcher bearers arrived.

Daylight was just breaking when we reached our minefield and listening post, and made it through to our own lines. It was great to be back.

The withdrawal was an outstanding success, all things considered. We got all of the wounded back except one. Poor old 'Papa' Jacobs was unconscious and we couldn't find him, but all the other 24 wounded we got back safely across the valley to our own lines. One of our wounded, Trevor Dick, later died in hospital and sometime later Racer Hill died as a result of his wounds.

The Canadian flak jacket that I wore during that operation without a doubt saved my life. After removing it to help my mate who was wounded, I had put it back on. When I got back to our line I took it off again and looked at it; it was completely shredded with shrapnel and bullets embedded. But all I got was slight bruising and welts around the midsection and back.

The Lord was with me, I reckon.

Throw Smoke –
I See Purple –
No I See Mauve!

Nev Modystack,
Royal Australian Armoured Corps, Vietnam

When a helicopter approached a landing zone (LZ) for whatever purpose, the standard procedure was for the controller of the LZ to throw a smoke grenade. He would then report to the aircraft that it had been thrown and asked the pilot to verify the colour. This was to ensure that the helicopter was in fact landing in the correct LZ and not an enemy trap.

On one occasion, 'Slim' Kennard was expecting a helicopter resupply and the following conversation ensued. (The call signs are false).

Pilot: Niner Foxtrot, this is Playboy Two Three, I'm inbound your loc, three minutes, throw smoke, over.

Slim: This is Niner Foxtrot, smoke thrown, over.

Pilot: I see purple, over.

Slim: Negative, negative, I threw mauve, over.

Pilot: Ah, well, I still see purple, over.

Slim: Roger, well that can't be my loc, out!

In Time for the News — From Lebanon to New York

Lieutenant Colonel Craig Kingston, UN Military Observer, Lebanon, 2000

Following the Israeli Defence Force (IDF) withdrawal from Southern Lebanon in May 2,000 after a 22-year occupation the situation was changing rapidly as the region adjusted to its new-found freedom and status. During this time there were still issues around where the border actually was and who was or wasn't on the right side of it.

During this period I was working in the region as UN Military Observer (UNMO) and our job was to report and observe on the situation including breaches of the relevant UN Security Resolution, number 425, of which there had been many, including several permanent breaches.

Due to force preservation issues UNMOs, who were unarmed, were not permitted to patrol during the hours of darkness. So it came as quite a surprise when my Operations Officer (OPSO) contacted me to undertake a new task. We were just about to close down for the evening as last light was rapidly approaching. I reminded him of the policy and he said that this was a high priority task that needed to be done and we had approval to work past last light. This was a first that I knew of for the mission.

The task involved travelling to a location known as Border Pillar (BP) 38 and report on the situation there. From our recent knowledge of visiting there we knew it to be an Israel Defence Force section outpost. We also knew that it was quite contentious where it actually was on the map. The maps issued by the UN were of dubious quality and relied on French information from around 1923. On a previous visit there the IDF Lieutenant in charge pulled out a more recent map and pointed out where he thought he was – which was clearly on the Israel side of the border — whereas the Lebanese contended they were on the their side of the border. Also at the time the Lieutenant kindly pointed out to us to be careful where we walked as his post was surrounded with unmarked minefields from previous campaigns.

So two UN colleagues, one of whom was serving his first day in the mission area and myself, set off for this unusual task keen to make use of the little remaining light. The problem with getting to BP 38 was that the road had been blocked to vehicle traffic at a distance of about 2 km. This meant the last 2 km were by foot. Again our Operations Officer was on the radio asking for an update, making it crystal clear in his thick Irish brogue we were to get a move on as he was copping all kinds of pressure from above.

As such we decided we had to run down to investigate. UN policy dictated that when outside of the vehicle on foot patrol we had to wear the blue UN flak jacket and helmet and carry a UN Flag. We also decided to take a pair of binoculars and a portable radio so we could call in from BP38 due to the urgency for information.

So two of us set off at a brisk pace, knowing we were running along a disputed border, carrying a strange ensemble of kit, on last light, in the middle of summer, with twitchy IDF troops on one side and uncertain Lebanese troops on the other, towards a location surrounded by unmarked minefields. My UN colleague, on his first day, was wondering what he had got himself in for.

Around ten minutes later and in fading light we arrived at the location. We conducted a thorough check of the location to discover that the IDF troops were no longer there. I then tried to raise the OPSO on the portable radio; however, I could not establish communication. As such we had to run back to use the more powerful vehicle radio. So off we set again running at a brisk pace in what was now total darkness. Our UN blue kit and flag was not of any protection for us now.

Upon arrival at the vehicle I raised the OPSO on the radio and informed him of the situation. He confirmed it three times. We then set off to return to the patrol base wondering what all the fuss was about and why the high priority. We arrived back and had our daily de-brief still bewildered by the last couple of hours' activities. We then showered and sat down for the evening meal around an hour later.

As was customary we switched on the TV to watch the daily news courtesy of CNN when there was a break in the scheduled program for a special live announcement from the Secretary-General of the UN, Kofi Annan.

Mr Annan, live from his UN Headquarters in New York, then came on the screen to announce that he had just been advised that the IDF withdrawal from Lebanon was now complete and that UN Security Council Resolution 425 had been fully complied with. It was at that point did the team realise why our task had been such a high priority.

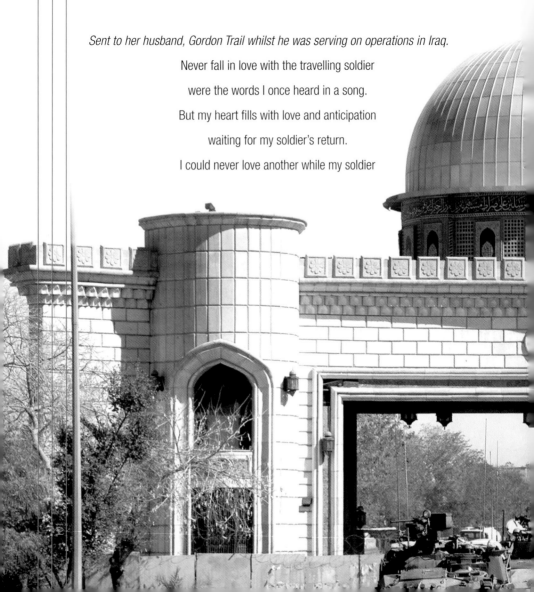

For My Husband

by Shona Traill

Sent to her husband, Gordon Trail whilst he was serving on operations in Iraq.

Never fall in love with the travelling soldier

were the words I once heard in a song.

But my heart fills with love and anticipation

waiting for my soldier's return.

I could never love another while my soldier

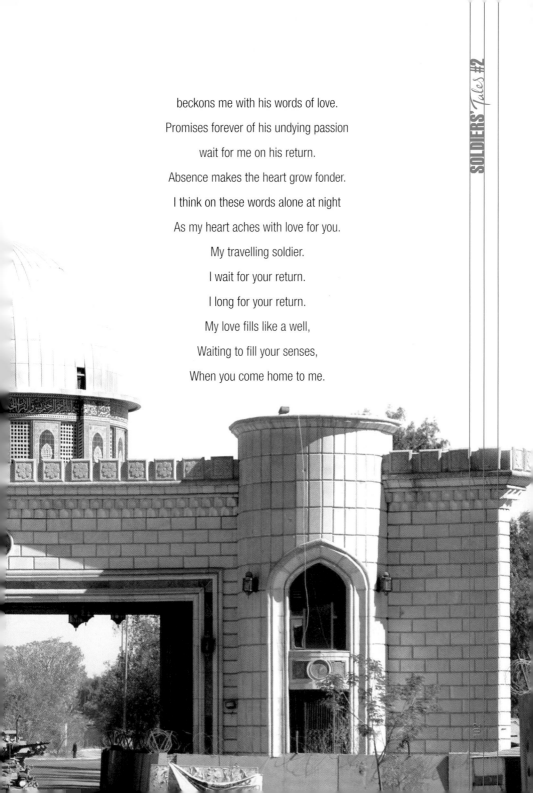

beckons me with his words of love.

Promises forever of his undying passion

wait for me on his return.

Absence makes the heart grow fonder.

I think on these words alone at night

As my heart aches with love for you.

My travelling soldier.

I wait for your return.

I long for your return.

My love fills like a well,

Waiting to fill your senses,

When you come home to me.

A Patrol in No Man's Land

Lieutenant John Adams,
MC, 54th Battalion, 1915
(then a Private in the 2nd Battalion)

Shortly after midday on the 5 May 1915, the 2nd Battalion moved off from behind Wire Gully to The Pimple, taking over the trenches there from the 2nd Brigade.

A few weeks later, General Walker, accompanied by some of his staff and our Commanding Officer Lieutenant Colonel Brown, came into our frontline, and pushing his oversized periscope – a stick with mirror top and bottom – over the top, noticed much digging activity by the Turks on the left of The Pimple. It appeared that the Turks were constructing a nearer line of trenches towards us. General Walker said to Colonel Brown: 'We must stop their caper. An officer and about 20 men would bag the lot, and if successful, of course, there would be honours so-and-so for the officer and honours so-and-so for the NCO and men.' We had all looked game enough until this remark was made. Everyone standing by became silent, no doubt turning over in his mind the thought that he might be one of the 'privileged' number. A singular thing, but all of us seemed to have an attack of coughing, until all 'the heads' departed. Immediately they left, Digger judges and juries unanimously condemned the idea.

On the morning of June 6, Sergeant H. Peisley, of A Company, came to me and said that I had been selected to go out on patrol in no man's land with him. The following day, Peisley and I had to report to Lieutenant Colonel Brown at battalion headquarters. After telling us what was required, he remarked, 'The principle of our patrol is to get the men used to seeing their own men patrolling no man's land in front of their barbed-wire. And whilst you are out, look about to see if the Turks are occupying any advanced positions at night. This information is required by General Walker.'

At 9.30 pm, Colonel Brown, the Adjutant, Captain Dingnam (our company commander), Peisley and myself assembled in the frontline near a sally port that had been specially made for our exit. The troops on both flanks had been warned that the patrol would be out for 40 minutes, and that firing was to cease for that time, or until such time as the patrol might possibly return.

After receiving final instructions from Colonel Brown, Peisley and I went out through the sally port. We had the devil's own job getting through our own wire entanglement, which had been cut into short lengths and thrown out haphazardly. The barbs caught in our clothes and flesh. Hundreds of Fray Bentos, Ticklers, and Maconache tins were lying about, and as we dragged lengths of wire over them, the noise resembled the beating of tins to frighten a swarm of bees. Getting beyond the line of wire, we freed each other out of these encumbrances, and began to crawl parallel to our frontline.

This, however, was not exciting enough for the game and fearless Peisley, who whispered that we should crawl side by side towards the Turkish line, he scanning the right and I the left. Sticking together, we got to within 50 yards of the Turkish position, when Peisley drew my attention to a rifle flash in our right rear. He whispered that if only one or two Turks were there, we had a chance of capturing them. After waiting a while, three or four more shots were fired from the same position. We scanned the horizon, and saw two heads, at which Peisley stopped me from firing.

Immediately the Turkish garrison seemed to become alarmed, for they opened up a hellish fire, to which our line retaliated. Bullets splashed the earth and scrub around us, and the Turks excitedly fired flares. With chin and nose dug into the earth, we waited motionlessly until at the end of 20 minutes the fusillade eased off. As Peisley remarked later, he thought we were there for keeps. The terror passed, and both became armed with venom for our men.

There was still a fair amount of firing; we returned to our line. Peisley's instinct took us back to the sally port, through which he could not scramble quickly enough to vent his feelings about the inconsiderate manner in which we had been 'baptised' in patrol work to Captain Dignam, and later to Colonel Brown and the battalion staff, all of whom had been anxiously waiting for our return. Peisley and I were informed that a few men on the right flank had become excited and started firing, and could not be induced to stop for some time. Peisley told the colonel that we would take the lot out.

Having each had our say, we came back to earth again, and gave Colonel Brown particulars of what we had seen. After being thanked and complimented upon the manner in which we had done the job, we retired to a communication trench. It all them seemed worthwhile.

A Lesson in Humility

Warrant Officer Class One John Sahariv, RAE

In 1969, I was posted to Papua New Guinea and was promoted to Sergeant not long after my arrival.

Being young and cocky and full of knowledge having been to the place in 1966, I was prepared to take on the world.

I had been to Vietnam on an army landing ship and gained my Vietnam Medal for being on active duty. I missed out by about three weeks for the second medal, the Vietnamese Campaign Medal, so effectively; I was classed by my mates as a 'SWINGER' not a 'CLANGER'.

Anyhow, one beautiful afternoon I was the Duty Sergeant at Murray Barracks. I was strutting about keeping a vigilant eye on the Pacific Islander (PI) Piquets when marching towards me, in starched juniper greens as crisp as a button, was, who I thought to be a PI Corporal with a splendidly polished black belt, brass keepers and boots, the badge on his beret shining brilliantly, and, lo and behold, wearing the Vietnam Medal and Vietnamese Campaign ribbons. A wonderful display of parade dress!

Wow. Here was my chance to make a name for myself; a PI wearing Vietnam Medal Ribbons? No PI's served in Vietnam, did they? NO!

I confronted the Corporal in broken Pidgin English, 'Corporal, where you kissum medal belong you?'

'Me gettim medal long Vietnam,' he replied.

To which I answered in the harshest voice I could muster, 'You lie; no PNG boy go fight long Vietnam!'

To which he replied, in a perfect Australian accent, 'You're right, Sarge, but I'm not a PI, I am an Aussie Aboriginal!'

I was so humiliated by my own eagerness to prove I was someone I wasn't, my arse hit the ground so hard I can still feel it today, 41 years later.

That was the first and last time I tried to big note myself.

We became friends he and I. He was promoted a few weeks later. However, over time we have lost contact and I have since heard that he may well have passed away.

A lesson learned at the right time in one's career can be a very beneficial lesson.

NX109319
2 Apr. Reay J.t.
No Aust. Commando
Sqn

Don't Drink that Water

On one patrol we came to a stream that wound around from behind a hill in front of us. Now dead Japs have a pretty foul smell and the air was thick with that smell. Anyway we washed our clothes, the only ones we owned, by jumping in the stream and brushing off the mud and rinsing the sweat off the rest of us. Some had a good drink out of the stream while others topped up their water bottles. We then proceeded around the hill where the water, about an inch in depth, was washing over the rocks. On the rocks was a dead Jap, bits of whom were flaking away into the water. Needless to say there was many a water bottle emptied and those who had drank him weren't too happy. Luckily I had neither drank the water or filled my bottle.

Nick Main, 2/2 Battalion, New Guinea, 1945

The Beirut Foreign Exchange

Les Tranter, 1st Battalion, the Royal Australian Regiment, United Nations Observer, Middle East, 1985–86

A normal day in Beirut in 1985–6 was not like a normal day in any other city on earth. Any number of artillery shells from a number of protagonists could rain on the city without warning or reason. Any number of the protagonists could be killed or injured, as could innocent citizens going about their daily business.

As such, life and business was different from elsewhere. At the time we were paid a mixture of both Lebanese currency and US dollars. It was necessary to do some currency exchange to the local currency for day-to-day life.

My money exchange was in downtown Hazmieyeh, the suburb where the Headquarters for the Observer Group, Beirut was located. I visited this office to do business. It consisted of a solid concrete cell about two metres wide by three deep, no windows, no back door, no skylight and accessed by only one very solid door. In an earlier life it was probably a small store-room. It was furnished with a small, single bare desk and chair.

All of which was bizarre enough but it was topped off by the fact that, sitting at the owner of this fine establishment's elbow, was a loaded and cocked AK47 and in the drawer, where he kept his cash, was a loaded and cocked Colt .45 automatic.

Such is the way business was done in this town at the time.

Captives of the Turk

Sergeant John Halpin,
12th Light Horse Regiment, Turkey, 1918

It was 1 May 1918 on the western side of the Jordan River, at a point 16 miles north of Jericho, and about one mile from its banks. The 4th Light Horse Brigade (consisting of the 4th Victorian, 11th Queensland and 12th NSW Regiments) had been allotted a frontage of two miles to prevent the Turk from advancing to the relief of Es Salt (a small village in the hills behind), known to be a Turkish stronghold and even then in the hands of others of our forces. We had taken up the position 24 hours previously. The first day was passed without incident. We were not much concerned with the isolated shots of hidden Bedouins as we watered our horses at a nearby stream. Throughout the night our thin line of outposts was not disturbed by a single shot, and at daylight we returned to the cover of a deep wadi, which effectively hid the whole of our unit, the 12th, every man, I am sure, felt that our job was a manageable one.

Most had obtained tinned foods at the canteen at Jericho to supplement the eternal ration of cheese and bacon. Sausages were sizzling in the mess-tin lids and billies boiling for the morning snack. I distinctly remember one man polishing his boots and leatherware, much to the disgust of the older hands. This was his first action, so probably as time went on he abandoned the niceties of peace-time soldiering.

It was probably eight o'clock when there was a scare and a stir. Our corporal had just returned from Brigade Headquarters. 'Jacko's over there in thousands,' he urged, pointing towards Jordan. Unofficially, he passed the word to all to get ready for quick movement. The increase of shell-fire searching us out in the wadi lent colour to his story, and most took him at his word and saddled up. Had we known the full force of circumstances we should have done so much more hurriedly. Almost at once orders were barked amid the tension which grips everyone when faced with the uncertainty of action, and within three minutes 'C' Squadron of the regiment was mounted to retire.

As we came to the mouth of the wadi, we took in the situation at a glance. Turks – 4,000 of them – were advancing towards us in eight extended lines and as we wheeled southward at the gallop, our flank was exposed to the fire of all arms. Our horses, sensing the danger, required no urge to cover the ground in the quickest possible time. We must have been a wonderful target, but the Turks, probably in their excitement, did not adjust the sights of their rifles, for the lead was passing harmlessly overhead. A confusion of impressions seem to struggle from consciousness when one is being fired at and cannot retaliate. That at least was my experience when my old roan neddy seemed to leap skyward suddenly, and just as suddenly I lost all interest in that retirement.

The sun was setting when I recovered a partial interest in things. Nobody was in sight, but, looking backwards at less than 200 yards, a small party of Turks was casually walking towards me. The sense of self-preservation was uppermost. Captivity did not enter my mind. Strange that of all possible eventualities, capture was never discussed in Palestine. It was as a thing that simply could not come to pass. Diggers are allegedly not given to prayer. I don't believe it, and venture the opinion that no deeper appeals have ascended to the Eternal Throne than from the silence of desperation in a soldier's heart… and I prayed.

Four Turks, now close at hand, saw me. One had a shot, but missed his target at less than 12 yards. The others had other intentions! In a twinkling I was stripped, and probably to avoid the envy of their comrades, my captors hid my articles of uniform beneath their own ragged garments, but one, more generous than the others, cast me a pair of cotton drawers tied at waist and ankles, and from there cut, intended exclusively for Mohammedan use.

My salvation lay in the early arrival of a Turkish officer, who disregarded my protests at my near nakedness, but made two of my captors carry me back to Turkish headquarters. A solitary figure standing on the hillock – General Liman Von Sanders, Commander-in-Chief of the Turkish Forces – was the centre of the wildest adulation of his officers and men, both German and Turk. Success had completely gone to their heads, and there was much evidence of that success. Already moving out for use against our forces were three brand new batteries of 13-pounder guns, captured intact from the Honourable Artillery Company, only a few hours previously. These guns had been in action for the first time, and the gun teams, a couple of weeks previously, had won all laurels for smartness and efficiency at a military gymkhana. Two armoured cars captured from us at the same time were being quickly requisitioned for the same mission as the guns. The full equipment of the 4th Brigade Field Ambulance and 25 prisoners, including 15 Australians, constituted truly, the biggest Turkish bag in the whole of his operations on any front.

As we stood by in silence, each filled with disrepair, a guttural command brought us back to earth – and Turkey. Instinctively we formed some semblance of a line, which included the wounded, already in a pitiable state. 'Did you receive orders to take no prisoners?' The words were spoken in broken English. The question was ominous, but in very truth we had received no such order and we told the interrogator so. 'Ah, that is good,' was the response of this big German officer. 'I was at one time Governor of German Samoa, and I know your country, Australia, well… Sydney and Melbourne…'

The Australians, grouped apart, seemed to move towards him, urged by this strange link with things which meant almost everything in life to us. He continued, '…But the war will soon be over for you… for us… our big offensive towards Paris… But you Australians, why did you come so far away to fight?'

Not a word was uttered in reply, for approaching us was the Commander-in-Chief himself. Wide-eyed, we gazed at this victor of the Gallipoli campaign. Tall, but sparsely built, with a slight stoop, he was almost indistinguishable in the simplicity of his uniform from the numerous officers of his retinue. One felt almost a sense of disappointment at this exemplar of the Prussian mailed fist, but when he spoke in accents of seeming friendliness, almost in tones of sympathy, it was hard to see in this man anything of the braggart or of ruthlessness.

He could not speak English, so to give us his message direct, spoke in French, which one of our number translated, 'You will not be prisoners very long… always have hope… Your action this morning failed because your strength was known. Four thousand Turkish soldiers have marched 12 miles overnight and have driven your forces back.' The anguished groans of a prisoner shot through both legs with machine-gun fire prompted the translator to ask the Commander-in-Chief that the wounded man be given relief. This was immediately ordered, and the poor chap was taken away, later to be released by our men in a Turkish hospital on their memorable advance. A complaint to the Commander-in-Chief that the Turks had robbed us of our clothing did not meet with the same success. Smilingly, he wagged his head in survey of our multi-coloured Turkish garb and moved off, doubtless too well versed on the 'taking' ways of his Turkish allies.

Thank God for Breaker Morant

Corporal George Mansford, 1st Battalion, the Royal Australian Regiment, Malaya 1960

After an attack of malaria and recovering at the British Military Hospital in Taiping I was sent to the Cameron Highlands to yet another British hospital for convalescence. My recovery had been quite quick and in a short time I became quite bored with the dull routine of a hospital environment and longed to be back with the platoon.

On the 24th of April during the daily ward inspection I suggested to Commanding Officer of the hospital that it would be a wonderful idea to give all the walking patients the opportunity to celebrate Anzac Day at the local kampong. He readily gave consent with the stipulation we were to be back in our ward by midday. I quickly agreed. Consequently on the morning of Anzac Day a group of us including Brits and Kiwis visited the local bar in the village and began to celebrate the one day of the year. We were well behaved and had every intention of not breaking our promise. Sadly we became victims yet again of poor communications between senior ranks.

Suddenly within our small group appeared the Regimental Sergeant Major of the hospital and he was clearly not in a good mood. He declared with much rage that we were out of bounds and to return to the hospital immediately. I pointed out the obvious but it was clear he was not interested in any agreements between colonials and his master. The outcome was that I refused to go and in a short time he and I were involved in a brawl.

As quick as a flash, or so it seems, the British Military Police arrived, arrested me and deposited me in the local civilian prison where I cooled my heels overnight.

The following morning I was fronted before the commanding officer, charged with several offences including striking a senior, and remanded to be served justice within my own battalion. Thus on my return to unit it seemed I was in disgrace and the company commander was far from pleased when he in turn remanded me to face the commanding officer of our battalion who was well known for his lack of sympathy when it came to discipline. The charges were serious and I was already preparing myself to remove the stripes from my shirt and perhaps even some time in the glass house commonly known in official military circles as detention. Then the miracle occurred.

The day before I was due to front our commanding officer, the weekly courier arrived with all the latest news form the outside world. Among the official signals was one concerning me and in a short time the company commander announced that a signal from the Commonwealth Brigade Headquarters advised that the charges against me had been dropped. The reason was that there had not been an Australian representative present during my arrest and thus it had been illegal and the truth was that such procedures had been implemented by the Australian Government shortly after Breaker Morant and his mate were executed by the British.

Thanks to Breaker Morant and Hitchcock, a subsequent miffed Australian Government and overenthusiastic British Military Police I was a free man. Breaker Morant and Hitchcock became my heroes and is it any wonder I never bother with Lotto I used up all my luck many years ago.

Despair on the Western Front

Where such tension exists in battle the rules of 'civilised' war are powerless. Most men are temporarily half mad, their pulses pounding at their ears, their mouths dry… When they have been wracked with machine gun fire, the routing out of enemy groups from behind several feet of concrete is almost inevitably the signal for a butchery at least of the first few who emerge, and sometimes even the helplessly wounded may not be spared… ruthlessness is a quality essential to hand-to-hand fighting, and soldiers were deliberately trained to it.

Charles Bean, Official War Historian, France 1917

Escape of a Timor Militiaman

Warrant Officer Class One Dave Trill, 2nd Battalion, the Royal Australian Regiment, Timor 1999

Soon after our short-notice call-out to East Timor in 1999, the 2nd Battalion went through its ritual of preparation lectures on the orders for opening fire, rules of engagement, laws of armed conflict, etc. These laws and rules are classified as restricted material, but suffice it to say there are some simple rules for this type of deployment and threat: we could not shoot someone without a weapon, nor could we fire warning shots, or shoot at an escapee.

With this in mind, two days after my arrival at Dili during the multinational peacekeeping operation International Force for East Timor (INTRERFET), we were in a defensive position around the airport buildings at Comoro. We stayed for one night prior to moving off the next day into a battalion headquarters position. During this time there was a steady collection of captured and detained militia being placed into the airport buildings, which were being used as a temporary holding facility. I remember looking at one who was a grubby bloke, with expectation in his eyes that these would probably be his last few moments on Earth, although this was not the case.

We were sitting around as we waited to move to our new position. More troops were still steadily pouring into Dili and the airport was becoming overcrowded. Our commanding officer decided we should get out of there sooner rather than later. Just as we were about to leave I heard some yelling from the western car park, where B Company were positioned. The 'grubby' militiaman had escaped custody and was moving faster than I've ever seen anyone move in his attempt to escape through our perimeter. I remember standing there with Sergeant (now Warrant Officer Class Two) Mick Rice saying, 'Look at this prick go!'

We watched with amusement as many of the rifle company soldiers in the area, fully aware of their orders about opening fire, pointed weapons and shouted warnings to try and stop this bloke, all to no avail. Some soldiers even resorted to chasing him, but with him in a t-shirt and shorts, and our blokes in webbing with weapons, there was not going to be any capture today unless this scared militiaman fell, or ran into someone! Most of the unit were laughing – some uncontrollably – at the speed of this bloke and the look of absolute fear on his face. All of this, combined with our hopeless attempt to catch him, made the situation pretty amusing during what was generally a stressful time (most of us were on our first operational tour).

Then, all of a sudden, shots were fired! Knowing the restrictions on opening fire most of the soldiers were amazed. As we looked around to where the shots came from the militiaman got away! I immediately looked at Mick and said, 'Mate, someone's in the shit here!' From the direction of the surprised soldiers who had just had a shot fired over their heads (or possibly through the position) came comments such as, 'Nice one, dickhead!', 'You weren't paying attention at the brief, were you, idiot?', and so on.

The bloke who fired the shot was found and 'verbally punched out' by the commanding officer. We then finally headed off on our way to our new position.

Kicked off the Chopper

Les Tranter, Anti-tank Platoon,
1st Battalion, the Royal Australian Regiment,
Vietnam 1968–69

Late in our tour the 1st Battalion, the Royal Australian Regiment (1RAR), occupied Fire Support Base 'Chestnut', around which we carried out a fairly intensive patrolling program for some time. We were scheduled to hand over to the 9th Battalion, the Royal Australian Regiment (9RAR) who were to continue the patrolling program, whilst we flew out to another area and onto another operation.

When we pulled out, Anti-tank Platoon was tasked with Pick-up Zone security for the day to protect the change over helicopter flights. It was to be a long day, staying switched on, making sure the fly in/out operation was not interrupted by any unwelcome attention from 'Charlie'.

Our Platoon Sergeant, Terry Schmidt, had set the soldiers into chopper loads (chalks). Anti-tank Platoon was scheduled to leave on the last flight out.

All went well throughout the day and the whole of 1RAR filtered through the Pick-up Zone and flown to our new area of operations. Whilst 9RAR flew in and moved into take up our old position at Fire Support Base 'Chestnut'.

As the choppers landed to take out the chalk before our own, the lead pilot signalled me over to his door and told me he had been allocated another task immediately after our flight. This meant he had to re-fuel before he picked us up for our journey. I gave him the thumbs up and off they went. I radioed battalion and told them our arrival would be delayed for a while due to the new tasking of the choppers. They acknowledged.

We settled down to wait, acutely aware that 'Charlie' now had ample time to pay our area a visit, to see what goodies he may be able to scrounge from the position we just evacuated.

The choppers returned without incident, and I stood at the last pad, watched the lads emplane, and their choppers get airborne. As the last to board I headed for the last chopper, sat on the floor and gave the thumbs-up to the pilot, who pulled pitch and headed off. The chopper tried to lift but was too heavy — one of the lads had gotten onto the last chopper instead of the second last, and the last was now over loaded and could not get airborne. We were a rather heavy platoon with all our normal gear, plus two dogs and a couple of 90mm Recoilless rifles and ammunition.

What do we do now, Batman?

Well what we do now is lighten the load, and to this end a big black door gunner leaned over and kicked me out! The chopper then headed off into the wild blue yonder.

There I was, 'on me Todd', and lonelier than a bastard on Father's Day!

Again, Batman, what do we do now? No means of communications, 'Charlie' likely to turn up at any minute and 9RAR in a new location and 'twitchy'. Not only that but I had no idea of their passwords, and half a kilometre or more to travel to reach their location.

So, very quietly and rather nervously, I set off, parallel to and 30 metres from, the fire-trail towards the 9th Battalion location. When I was about 150–100 metres short of the battalion position I stepped out onto the middle of the fire-trail, raised both arms and with my rifle held high above my head commenced to sing 'Waltzing Matilda' and barrack loudly for Geelong, (I thought, briefly, that I might barrack for Collingwood, but then considered that was a sure way of drawing fire!!).

Much to the amusement of the 9RAR sentries they let me in, and the Duty Officer graciously called my battalion headquarters on the blower, who sent our Direct Support chopper back to pick me up.

I arrived home to our new location safe and sound, and other than an aching sphincter, none the worse for wear — although the boys gave me a shellacking for some time.

The Missing Crate of Beer

It was not all fighting and dying. Sometimes we were on reserve, which meant we had to do odd jobs. One July night in 1945 we had to unload a beer barge packed with large crates of beer and also the more sophisticated stuff for the officers. There were security guards all over the place and large lights to see that the stuff did not go astray. The trucks drove right onto the barge to be loaded. Now we could not let all this beer slip past us could we? So in the shadow of the crates we gradually emptied one of them by slipping bottles under our shirts and then hanging on to the bottom of the trucks as they drove off. Then as they drove off into the night we would drop off, hide the bottles then saunter back onto the barge for more. In this way we cleaned out an entire crate plus a smaller one of cherry brandy destined for the officers. I don't know what the guards thought when they found the empty crates but for a few nights after that the jungle air reverberated to the sounds of jolly merriment.

Nick Main, 2/2 Battalion, New Guinea, 1945

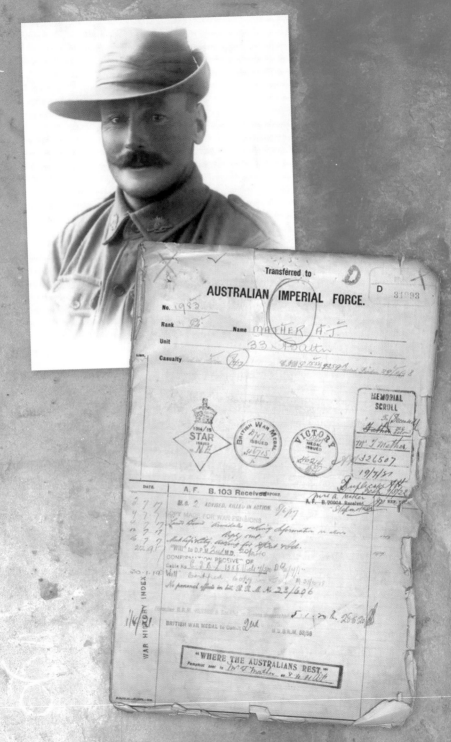

A Son Found

In November of 1930, a news item appeared in the Broken Hill Barrier Miner

AFTER 14 YEARS

Body of Missing Soldier Found at Pozieres

Mrs R. Mahoney received word today that her son's body had been found after 14 years. The Imperial War Graves Commission had informed that the remains of an Australian officer and eight soldiers had been recovered from an isolated grave near Pozieres. Among those recovered was her son. The shock, after so many years of anxiety as to what had happened to her eldest boy, prostrated Mrs Mahoney. Her son, who was 20 when he enlisted in 1915, was reported missing on 5 August 1916.

Mrs Emma Clark of Wilcannia attached this same newspaper clipping along with her letter to the army in the hope that her missing son might be among those found.

Dear Sir

I am enclosing a small slip of paper I cut out of the Broken Hill Barrier Miner saying that an Australian soldier's body had been found with others. Would you kindly try and find out if my son, Private Joseph Clark, 7th Reinforcements 45 Battalion No 2876 who enlisted from Wilcannia was amongst them? He left Australia in 1916 and was only seven months away when I got a cable to say he was wounded. Later I got another cable to say 'missing and wounded'. Then later I got a cable to say 'killed in action'. I could never find out if my little boy's body was ever found. It was in June he was reported killed. He was not 23 years old. Do please try and find out if his dear body is amongst those found and you will oblige his anxious mother.

It was a forlorn hope. Private Clark had been killed at Messines in 1917 and many miles from the killing fields of Pozieres.

The commitment to honour Australia's war dead, to care for the existing cemeteries and, very occasionally now, to identify the remains of Australian soldiers, continues undiminished to this day. The words of Emma Clark give a small glimpse of the pain endured by thousands of families, especially those whose loved ones who remain listed as 'missing'.

On 22 July 2010 Private Alan James Mather of the 33rd Australian Infantry Battalion was reburied with his mates in a newly marked grave near where he fell 93 years earlier on 7 June 1917 in the battle of Messines, the very same battle which claimed Emma Clark's son. Private Mather's body was discovered in 2008 during an archaeological dig in what was, in 1917, the infamous Ploegsteert Wood. Private Mather was one of the 6,178 Australian men killed in action, with no known grave from World War I, and one of 54,896 soldiers who lost their lives on the Western Front. He was finally laid to rest, buried, with full military honours — a moving and highly symbolic moment.

Although the pain has diminished, the passage of years makes identification a difficult task. The effort and expense devoted to finding and notifying relatives, to providing the honour of burial and the dignity of a marked grave are signs that our nation will not only keep faith with the relatives of our war dead, but that we will give true meaning to the words 'lest we forget'. Emma Clark has long since passed away, but her words remind us of the terrible cost of war.

As for Private Clark, the officer in charge of base records was able to respond to his mother that his body had indeed been found. While that knowledge must have released her from her lonely vigil, we are left to wonder how she coped with the further pain that his letter inadvertently inflicted on a heart already broken in that it was sent to the father some seven years prior to her letter.

Dear Madam

I have to advise that the remains of your son, the late No. 2876 Private J. Clark, 45th Battalion, are interred in Plot 5, Row 'A' Grave 21 of Wytschaete Military Cemetery. Mr Richard Clark, the deceased's Father, was notified to this effect on 27.4.23.

The Fuzzy Wuzzy Angels

Sapper H 'Bert' Beros,
7th Division, AIF, New Guinea

Many a mother in Australia, when the busy day is done,

Sends a prayer to the Almighty for the keeping of her son.

Asking that an angel guide him and bring him safely back,

Now we see those prayers are answered on the Owen Stanley track.

For they haven't any halos, only holes slashed in the ears,

And with faces worked by tattoos, with scratch pins in their hair.

Bringing back the wounded, just as steady as a hearse,

Using leaves to keep the rain off and as gentle as a nurse.

Slow and careful in bad places, on the awful mountain track,

And the look upon their faces, makes us think that Christ was black.

Not a move to hurt the carried, as they treat him like a saint,

It's a picture worth recording, that an artist's yet to paint.

Many a lad will see his mother, and the husbands, weans and wives,

Just because the Fuzzy Wuzzy carried them to save their lives.

From mortar or machine gun fire, or a chance surprise attack,

To safety and the care of doctors, at the bottom of the track.

May the mothers in Australia, When they offer up a prayer,

Mention those impromptu Angels, with the Fuzzy Wuzzy hair.

Smoke and Mirrors

Nev Modystack,
Royal Australian Armoured Corps, Vietnam

Smoking in armoured fighting vehicles (AFVs) is *verboten* for many a good reason.

Scene: Briefing by the Squadron Commander before an exercise: 'Remember that smoking on the vehicles is not allowed.'

Interim: Troop Leader makes an acronym for returning to base; 'PUF-O' this translates to Pack Up and F… Off!

Later: Squadron Commander radios 'All stations, this is niner, end of exercise, return to base, out.' Troop Leader on his troop net: 'All stations One, PUF-O, out.'

Squadron Commander — listening in: 'If I catch anyone, I say again anyone smoking on AFVs I will charge them myself!'

The Critic

The Australian soldier was not an unfair critic. If the performance of a neighbouring unit excited his admiration, no one was so enthusiastic and outspoken in his praise; but, where performance fell short of its expectations, it was quite useless to attempt to gloss over to him such failure. He founded his opinion upon what he himself saw. And, whether his view was favourable or unfavourable, he expressed it, whenever the subject arose, with the freedom that had been his right and habit from childhood.

Charles Bean, Official War Historian, France 1918

UNIDENTIFIED
AUSTRALIAN SOLDIER
1942-43

WX Unknown

Sapper H 'Bert' Beros,
7th Division, AIF, New Guinea

We knew he came from the Western State, Though to us he remained unknown;
For the WX was marked in his hat — The rest a mortar had blown.

We buried him there, on the mountain spur, where the trees are draped in moss;
We thought of his mother, no news for her of that irreplaceable loss.

Just a boy he looked, with his snowy hair, As we laid him down in the clay;
The padre's voice was low and clear, No others had words to say.

Yet we knew a mother would watch and wait, for a letter sent by her boy, How she
would dream of the things he did, How his first words caused her joy

And as he went off to school or game, he'd wave her fond goodbyes. Just as he did
when the great call came, And the hot tears hurt her eyes.

Perhaps she will know in some unknown way, Of that little rugged cross, The
remains of her hero beneath it lay, Where the trees are draped in moss.

We cursed the foe, who stripped the dead, No pity on them can be shown.
We marked his cross so it can be read, 'WX' Unknown.

Cats and Canadians: Titti La Hogue

Major Peter Beale, 9th Royal Tank Regiment, Normandy (now bona fide Aussie)

The 9th Royal Tank Regiment supported the Canadians in the battles of early August 1944 when they attempted to reach Falaise to close the 'Gap'. All of the area immediately south of Caen, from where the Canadians started, had been heavily bombed over several weeks; one of the villages in the area was La Hogue.

The 'green fields' referred to relate to the colours of the Royal Tank Regiment flag, brown, red, and green. This describes the path of a tank through mud and blood to the green fields beyond. When a tankman was killed he was said to enter the green fields.

Although the village of La Hogue had been very heavily bombed, there was still life, as Cyril Smith remembers: 'We moved back round Caen and entered La Hogue after it had been erased by a heavy bomber raid. At that time I was the wireless-op in Impulse, the troop sergeant's tank in 9 Troop B Squadron. Out of the rubble came a distressed tiny black and white kitten. We took it on board, to be attended to later. After bivouacking down for the night we examined it and found it to be a tom. He was too young to take any solid food, and had to be given liquid through a rubber tube. Consequently he was named Titti la Hogue, and signed on as spare crew.

'This little cat became a great inspiration to us in the art of survival. He would never leave the vicinity of the tank. He may have lost his hearing, because noise never bothered him. Titti went through many escapades with us. His place was sitting on the tool box behind the driver or in the co-driver's pannier bin. Only once did he get too near the clutch pedal, but fortunately squawked a warning in time.

'One morning in a flax field in Belgium Titti was missing. We decided he had been taken prisoner by either friend or foe. We found him later, but didn't put him on a charge. Instead he had a double ration of sardines and machonochy's soup with a good rollicking.

'Unfortunately some weeks later it became Titti's turn to enter the green fields. His eyes became badly affected with some type of liquid, possibly acid, giving him great pain. We had to administer an overdose of chloroform, and buried him at the side of a canal in Holland. It gave us great sadness, knowing that we had lost a faithful crew member. His ninth life ended as a tankie.'

Titti was not the only kitten found and rescued in this area. Ginger Gadd was in 5 Troop of A Squadron, a crew member in the tank of the troop leader Gerry 'The Gaffer' Wells.

'It was about the time of the Falaise Gap. We were stretched out along the road waiting to move forward, and everywhere there were signs "Achtung Minen" and "Keep off the verges". Suddenly this little bundle of fur appeared, black as night and so cute and lovely that I couldn't bear to think of it getting blown into the next world before its time. We tried all ways to get the kitten off the verge and at long last succeeded. The question then was what are we going to call it. After much deliberation we decided that because she had had such a timely escape from explosives we would call her "Nitro". She used to sleep alright whether the guns were firing or not.'

Cricket on the Somme

'Spider' Webb was a Cockney — from Stepney, I believe — who was with us on the Somme in 1916. He was a splendid cricketer.

We had had a very stiff time for six or seven hours and were resting during a lull in the firing. Then suddenly Jerry sent over five shells. After a pause another shell came over and burst near to Spider and his two pals.

When the smoke cleared I went across to see what had happened.

Spider's two pals were beyond help. The Cockney was propping himself up with his elbows surveying the scene.

'What's happened, Webb?' I said.

'Blimey! What's happened?' was the reply. 'One over – two bowled' (and, looking down at his leg) – 'and I'm stumped.'

Then he fainted.

Lieutenant George Franks, MC, Royal Artillery, Somme

The Highest Honour — For Valour

The Victoria Cross is the pre-eminent award for acts of bravery in wartime and is Australia's highest military honour. It is awarded to persons who, in the presence of the enemy, display the most conspicuous gallantry; a daring or pre-eminent act of valour or self-sacrifice; or extreme devotion to duty.

The last three Australians to be awarded the Victoria Cross are Keith Payne, VC, OAM; Mark Donaldson, VC; and Benjamin Robert-Smith, VC, MG.

Warrant Officer Class Two Keith Payne, VC, OAM

Becoming a VC holder is a responsibility; you become public property, but you can inspire people.

I was in the army 19 years before I saw a Victoria Cross for the first time and that was when the Queen gave me mine.

It was my responsibility to get as many soldiers out of that battle field as possible. It was my responsibility.

Was I afraid? My God yes, yes, I was. But it's your job, you've got to do it and you get on with it. You try not to think about being frightened, you know.

On 24 May 1969 Payne was commanding the 212th Company of the 1st Mobile Strike Force Battalion in the Kontum province, South Vietnam, when the battalion was attacked by a numerically superior North Vietnamese force. The two forward companies were heavily attacked with rockets, mortars and machine-guns from three directions simultaneously. The indigenous soldiers faltered so Payne rushed about firing his Armalite rifle and hurling grenades to keep the enemy at bay while he tried to rally the soldiers. In doing so he was wounded in the hands, upper arm and hip by four pieces of rocket shrapnel and one piece of mortar shrapnel.

The battalion commander decided to fight his way back to base and this movement commenced by the only available route. With a few remnants of his company, which had suffered heavy casualties, Payne covered the withdrawal with grenades and gunfire and then attempted to round up more of his company. By nightfall he had succeeded in gathering a composite party of his own and another company and had established a small defensive perimeter about 350 metres north-east of the hill. The enemy by now had captured the former hill-top position.

In darkness Payne set off to locate those who had been cut off and disoriented. At 9 pm (2100hrs) he crawled over to one displaced group, having tracked them by the fluorescence of their footsteps in rotting vegetable matter on the ground, and thus began a 800 metre traverse of the area for the next three hours. The enemy were moving about and firing, but Payne was able to locate some forty men, some wounded, some of whom Payne personally dragged out. He organised others who were not wounded to crawl out on their stomachs with wounded on their backs.

Once he concentrated his party he navigated them back to the temporary perimeter only to find the position abandoned by troops who had moved back to the battalion base. Undeterred he led his party, as well as another group of wounded encountered enroute, back to the battalion base where they arrived at about 3 am (0300hrs).

Corporal Mark Donaldson, VC

I don't see myself as a hero. I was in Afghanistan just doing my job. My training and my instincts took over on the day.

It is a great honour. But in the long run I just want to go back to being a soldier because that is what I joined the army to do.

I just saw him there so I went over to get him. There was a lot of fire coming down. You could see it kicking up everywhere in the dust around us. It was pretty intense. I started dragging him first, then got him to his feet, got my arm under him and back to the relative safety of the vehicle.

I didn't really have time to think about it. I was too busy worrying about getting back to my mates and getting us all through it.

On 2 September 2008, during the conduct of a fighting patrol, Corporal (then Trooper) Donaldson was travelling in a combined Afghan, US and Australian vehicle convoy that was engaged by a numerically superior, entrenched and coordinated enemy ambush. The ambush was initiated by a high volume of sustained machine gun fire coupled with the effective use of rocket propelled grenades. Such was the effect of the initiation that the combined patrol suffered numerous casualties, completely lost the initiative and became immediately suppressed. It was over two hours before the convoy was able to establish a clean break and move to an area free of enemy fire.

In the early stages of the ambush, Corporal Donaldson reacted spontaneously to regain the initiative. He moved rapidly between alternate positions of cover engaging the enemy with 66mm and 84mm anti-armour weapons as well as his M4 rifle. During an early stage of the enemy ambush, he deliberately exposed himself to enemy fire in order to draw attention to himself and thus away from wounded soldiers. This selfless act alone bought enough time for those wounded to be moved to relative safety.

As the enemy had employed the tactic of a rolling ambush, the patrol was forced to conduct numerous vehicle manoeuvres, under intense enemy fire, over a distance of approximately four kilometres to extract the convoy from the engagement area. Compounding the extraction was the fact that casualties had consumed all available space within the vehicles. Those who had not been wounded, including Corporal Donaldson, were left with no option but to run beside the vehicles throughout.

During the conduct of this vehicle manoeuvre to extract the convoy from the engagement area, a severely wounded coalition force interpreter was inadvertently left behind. Of his own volition and displaying complete disregard for his own safety, Corporal Donaldson moved alone, on foot, across approximately 80 metres of exposed ground to recover the wounded interpreter. His movement, once identified by the enemy, drew intense and accurate machine gun fire from entrenched positions. Upon reaching the wounded coalition force interpreter, Corporal Donaldson picked him up and carried him back to the relative safety of the vehicles then provided immediate first aid before returning to the fight.

Corporal Benjamin Roberts-Smith, VC, MG

My head's still spinning. It feels extremely humbling and makes me feel extremely proud to be a part of the unit, but more so the squadron for what we achieved on the day and being a part of something where we took the fight to the Taliban and we won. The boys did some amazing things.

I was just like everyone else in Afghanistan; I was doing my job – I know it's a cliché but it's true. You always go over there and fight as hard you can and never go over there half-hearted.

Every single guy in that troop at some stage was fighting for his life; there were a lot of brave men doing a lot of brave things.

We got back to the base that night with dirt and blood on our uniforms and had a pie. Thirty minutes later we went to bed, got up the next day and went on another mission that night. That's just how it was.

On 11 June 2010, a troop of the Special Operations Task Group conducted a helicopter assault into Tizak, Kandahar Province, in order to capture or kill a senior Taliban commander.

Immediately upon the helicopter insertion, the troop was engaged by machine gun and rocket propelled grenade fire from multiple, dominating positions. Two soldiers were wounded in action and the troop was pinned down by fire from three machine guns in an elevated fortified position to the south of the village. Under the cover of close air support, suppressive small arms and machine gun fire, Corporal Roberts-Smith and his patrol manoeuvred to within 70 metres of the enemy position in order to neutralise the enemy machine gun positions and regain the initiative.

Upon commencement of the assault, the patrol drew very heavy, intense, effective and sustained fire from the enemy position. Corporal Roberts-Smith and his patrol members fought towards the enemy position until, at a range of 40 metres, the weight of fire prevented further movement forward. At this point, he identified the opportunity to exploit some cover provided by a small structure.

As he approached the structure, Corporal Roberts-Smith identified an insurgent grenadier in the throes of engaging his patrol. Corporal Roberts-Smith instinctively engaged the insurgent at point-blank range resulting in the death of the insurgent. With the members of his patrol still pinned down by the three enemy machine gun positions, he exposed his own position in order to draw fire away from his patrol, which enabled them to bring fire to bear against the enemy. His actions enabled his Patrol Commander to throw a grenade and silence one of the machine guns. Seizing the advantage, and demonstrating extreme devotion to duty and the most conspicuous gallantry, Corporal Roberts-Smith, with a total disregard for his own safety, stormed the enemy position killing the two remaining machine gunners.

His act of valour enabled his patrol to break into the enemy position and to lift the weight of fire from the remainder of the troop who had been pinned down by the machine gun fire. On seizing the fortified gun position, Corporal Roberts-Smith then took the initiative again and continued to assault enemy positions in depth during which he and another patrol member engaged and killed further enemy. His acts of selfless valour directly enabled his troop to go on and clear the village of Tizak of Taliban. This decisive engagement subsequently caused the remainder of the Taliban in Shah Wali Kot District to retreat from the area.

Corporal Roberts-Smith's most conspicuous gallantry in a circumstance of extreme peril was instrumental to the seizure of the initiative and the success of the troop against a numerically superior enemy force. His valour was an inspiration to the soldiers with whom he fought alongside and is in keeping with the finest traditions of the Australian Army and the Australian Defence Force.

Acknowledgments

Page No.	Story	Photo Source	Photo Description	Story Source
1-2	A Tearful Thank You	AWM ART40573	Fletcher, Bruce, Landing at Duc Thanh, oil on canvas on hardboard, 102.6 x 133.1 cm	Lieutenant Dave Sabben, MG
3-6	A Humble Lieutenant	Charles Granquist	Turkish POWs at Torbruk.	Charles Granquist
7-8	The Last Rose of Ypres	AWM E01117	View of the ruins of the Cloth Hall and the Cathedral at Ypres, 1917.	Frank Hurley
9-10	Left Out In No Man's Land	AWM P01630.002	No. 2 Australian General Hospital, Wimereux, France C.1918	Sister Margaret Dorothy Edis, interview for the Oral History Programme by Vicky Hobbs and Shelley Gare, 25 July 1975, J.S. Battye Library of West Australian History, Perth.
11-15	Last Men Standing	Photo 1: AWM E03649. Photo 2: Damien Finlayson.	Photo 1: 1st Australian Tunnelling Company men with French villager Nord Region (France), Busigny, 1918. Photo 2: Jim Savage and mates.	Damien Finlayson
15-22	Anzac Day in Baghdad	Marcus Fielding	Photo 1: Baghdad War Cemetery. Photo 2: Soldiers Salute during Anzac Day service. Photo 3: Author in front of Baghdad War Cemetery. Photo 4: Soldiers secure Baghdad War Cemetery.	Colonel Marcus Fielding

Page No.	Story	Photo Source	Photo Description	Story Source
23-26	Taken Prisoner at Fleurbaix	Chalk collection courtesy David Coombes	German POW camp.	William Charles Barry, Personal Diary entry. Part of the Chalk papers at University of Tasmania
27-28	Low Flying Aircraft	Art by Jeff Isaac	Photo 1: Japanese Fighter Nakajima Ki-43 Hayabusa (Oscar) Photo 2: Japanese Fighter, Mitsubishi A6M2 Reisen (Zero).	Corporal Brian Murray, first published, Khaki and Green, With the Australian Army at Home and Overseas, The Australian War Memorial,1943, p.86
29-32	Letters from Timor	Graeme Ramsden	Photo 1&2: Chaplain Ramsden with the kids from the orphanage at Laga. Photo 3: Huts in the village of Pefentil, Timor 2000.	Chaplain Graeme Ramsden
33-38	You Don't Let Your Mates Down	Craig Deayton	Photos 1,2,4: Reg Lawler. Photo 3: Water Fight Reg Lawler and Mick Deayton	Craig Deayton
39-42	Nothing Worthwhile Doing Comes Without Sacrifice	Photo 1&2: Department of Defence. Photo 3: James Fanning	Photo 1: SF Soldiers in Afghanistan, 2011, Photo 2: Soldiers of the 6th Battalion, the Royal Australian Regiment prepare for a patrol. Photo 3: James Fanning Platoon on the Pirate Ship, Dah Rawood Afghanistan, 2011.	Lieutenant James Fanning, DSM

Page No.	Story	Photo Source	Photo Description	Story Source
43-44	The Agony of Killing	AWM ART40503	Fletcher, Bruce; Truong Van Nghe, Black and brown fibre-tipped pen on paper, 1967	Direct from author —Anonymous
45-50	The Bloke with the Pink Top	Photo 1&3: James Hurst, Photo 2: AMW ART02873	Photo 1: The Pink Tops Stand in Perth. Photo 2: Lambert, George; Anzac, the landing 1915, Oil on canvas, 1920-1922. Photo 3: Grave of David Simcock, Perth.	James Hurst
51-52	Swing Low, Sweet Chariot	AWM HOBJ2082	Having chased Chinese forces out of a tough patch of hilly country (near Hill 614) in Central Korea, these stretcher bearers of 3rd Battalion, the Royal Australian Regiment, carry out their casualties, South Korea, 1951.	Private Eric Donnelly
53-58	Training the Bodes	Art by Terry Smith	Drawing of Cambodian soldiers.	Terry Smith
59	Trimmed or Cut	AWM 020494	Shaving on the frontline, Tobruk, 1941	Major General John Joseph Murray
61-66	A Scotsman Always Pays a Debt	Photo 1: AWM E00771, Photo 2: AWM E03971	Photo1: Two unidentified water carriers of the 47th Battalion, AIF, near 'Albania', Ypres, 1917. Photo 2: An old ditch turned into a trench which was an objective in the attack on Fromelles on 19 July 1916.	Reg A. Watson

Page No.	Story	Photo Source	Photo Description	Story Source
67-68	They Are Just Like You	AWM SHA/66/0007/VN	Troops of The 1st Battalion, the Royal Australian Regiment (1RAR, Vietnam 1966.	Private Ian Cavanough
69-72	A Soldier's Flower	Photo 1: AWM 003742 Photo 2: AWM ART23390 Photo 3: AWM P05555	Photo 1: Puckapunyal Barracks 1940. Photo 2: Buckmaster, Ernest; Section of camp at 1 Base Ordnance Depot, Bandiana, Oil on canvas, 1945. Photo 3: Members of 2/22nd Battalion, outside barracks at Puckapunyal, 1940.	Corporal William O'Neill
73-74	Moya Moya	AWM ART 02811	Lambert, George; The Charge of the Australian Light Horse at Beersheba, 1917, Oil on canvas, 1920	Henry Gullet, first published Khaki and Green, With the Australian Army at Home and Overseas, The Australian War Memorial,1943.
75-78	The Landing: First Clash with Turks	Photo 1: AWM C01890 Photo 2: AWM P0287.11	Photo 1&2: Australian troops being towed ashore in lighters to land at Anzac Cove, April, 1915.	William Cridland first published, Revelle 1930.
79-80	Hell's Orchestra, Polygon Wood	AMW E01402	The 30th Battalion in the forward area trenches near Zonnebeke, in the Ypres Sector, 1917.	Captain Alexander Ellis. The story of the Fifth Australian Division, being an authoritative account of the division's doings in Egypt, France and Belgium. London, Hodder and Stoughton limited, pp244-5

Page No.	Story	Photo Source	Photo Description	Story Source
81-82	Lucky Miss from an IED	Department of Defence	Members of 6th Battalion, the Royal Australian Regiment patrolling in Uruzgan Province, Afghanistan, 2011.	Corporal Adam Marsh
83-84	Water and Garbage Run at Nui Dat	AWM MISC/66/0027/VN	The kitchen belonging to the 1st Australian Logistic Support Group Vung Tau, Vietnam. 1966.	Corporal Dave Morgan
85-86	A Medic in the Battle of Lone Pine	Private Collection	Wallace Anderson and Lousi McCubbin, Battle of Lone Pine, Diarama.	Private Edward Joseph Smalley, first published in the History of the 3rd Battalion AIF
87-90	The Tobruk Standard	Photo 1: AWM P00426.005 Photo 2: AWM 020761	Photo 1: J. Smith of the 2/17th battalion standing at the grave of Corporal John Edmondson, VC, of the same unit, in the Tobruk War cemetery, 1941. Photo 2: Men of the 2/13th Australian Infantry Battalion digging in, Tobruk, 1941.	General John Joseph Murray
91-94	Operation Buffalo	Photo 1: AWM HOBJ4489 Photo 2: AWM HOBJ1625	Photo 1: The 2nd Battalion, the Royal Australian Regiment, start carrying their ammunition off The Hook to a reserve company position. Korea, 1953. Photo 2: Troops of the 3rd Battalion, the Royal Australian Regiment, entering Pakchon, North Korea, 1950.	Eddie Wright

Page No.	Story	Photo Source	Photo Description	Story Source
95-96	Throw Smoke – I See Purple – No I See Mauve!	AWM ART40647	McFadyen, Ken; RAAF No. 9 Squadron, Iroquois helicopter resupply to forward company on patrol, Charcoal, rubbing out on paper, November 1967.	Nev Modystack
97-100	In Time for the News – From Lebanon to New York	Craig Kingston	UN observers and observations posts in Lebanon, 2000.	Lieutenant Colonel Craig Kingston
101-102	For My Husband	Department of Defence.	Security Detachment XII, Iraq, 2001.	Shona Traill
103-106	A Patrol in No Man's Land	Photo1: Jeff Isaacs, Photo 2: AWM G00267	Photo 1: Jeff Isaacs drawing Australian trench Gallipoli. Photo 2: Two soldiers cutting up barbed wire for jam tin bombs. Gallipoli, 1915.	Lieutenant John Adams, first published Revelle 1930
107-108	A Lesson in Humility	AWM BEL/69/0741/VN	Caribou aircraft used to air-lift Australian troops from the field to their Nui Dat base. South Vietnam, 1969.	Warrant Officer Class One John Sahariv
109-110	Don't Drink that Water	AWM ART25752	Hele, Ivor; Trooper Jack Reay, Pencil on paper, 1944	Nick Main
111-112	The Beirut Foreign Exchange	Les Tranter	Photo 1: Ruined building in Beirut.	Les Tranter
113-118	Captives of the Turk	Photo 1: AWM B01468, Photo 2: AWM P00339.025	Photo 1: 1st Australian Light Horse Brigade, Jericho Feb 18. Photo 2: Australian Light Horse, after first battle of Amman, Palestine, 1918.	Sergeant John Halpin, first published in Revelle 1930.

Page No.	Story	Photo Source	Photo Description	Story Source
119-120	Thank God for Breaker Morant	Private collection	Breaker Morant.	Corporal George Mansford
121-122	Despair on the Western Front	AWM E03864	Dead and wounded Australians and Germans in the railway cutting on Broodseinde Ridge, in the Ypres sector, in Belgium, during the battle of Passchendaele, on October 12, 1917.	Charles Bean, The AIF in France 1917, Volume IV, The Official History of Australia in the War of 1914–1918, Sydney, 1941, p.624
123-126	Escape of Timor Militia	Photo 1: AWM ART91105. Photo 2. Department of Defence.	Photo 1: Amor, Rick; Rural destruction, Oil on canvas, Timor, 1999-2000. Photo 2: Soldiers conducting road in Timor.	Warrant Officer Class One Dave Trill
127-130	Kicked Off the Chopper	AWM EKN/67/0130/VN	Members of B Company, 7th Battalion, the Royal Australian Regiment, just north of the village of Phuoc Hai.	Les Tranter
131-132	The Missing Crate of Beer	AWM ART22739	Hodgkinson, Roy; Barge landing, Oro Bay, New Guinea, Black and sanguine crayon with coloured washe on paper, 1942.	Nick Main

Page No.	Story	Photo Source	Photo Description	Story Source
133-136	A Son Found	Photo 1&2: Private collection. Photo 3&4: Department of Defence.	Photo 1: Private Mather. Photo 2: Private Mather medals. Photo 3&4: Australian Army Honour Guard lay Private Mather to rest at Prowse Point Military Cemetery, Ploegsteert, Belgium, July 2010.	Craig Deayton
137-138	The Fuzzy Wuzzy Angels	AWM 013993	Wounded being brought in on stretchers along a track through the kunai grass. The bearers are Papuan Natives, fondly known as Fuzzy Wuzzy Angels. Buna, 1942.	Sapper H 'Bert' Beros
139-140	Smoke and Mirrors	Private collection	Centurion tank.	Nev Modystack
141-142	The Critic	AWM P00437.017	Soldiers walk along the path beside the row of front line trenches, Fleurbaix, France, 1916.	Charles Bean, The AIF in France 1917, Volume IV, The Official History of Australia in the War of 1914–1918, Sydney, 1941.
143-144	WX Unknown	AWM 054554	Unidentified Soldiers at the Soputa War Cemetery. Soputa, New Guinea, 1943.	Sapper H 'Bert' Beros
145-148	Cats and Canadians: Titti La Hogue	Peter Beale	Photo 1&3: Chruchills at Norrey in Bessin June 1944. Photo 2: Crew of 9 Troop Leader's tank, Belgium, April 1945	Major Peter Beale

Page No.	Story	Photo Source	Photo Description	Story Source
149-150	Cricket on the Somme	AWM E01220	Five Australians passing along a duckboard track over mud and water among gaunt bare tree trunks in the devastated Chateau Wood, Ypres, 1917.	George Franks
151-160	The Highest Honour — For Valour	Department of Defence	Photo 1: Keith Payne, VC, OAM. Photo 2: Mark Donaldson, VC. Photo 3: Benjamin Roberts-Smith, VC, MG	Courtesy of Defence, Keith Payne, VC, OAM, Mark Donaldson, VC, Benjamin Roberts-Smith, VC, MG

OTHER TITLES BY THIS AUTHOR

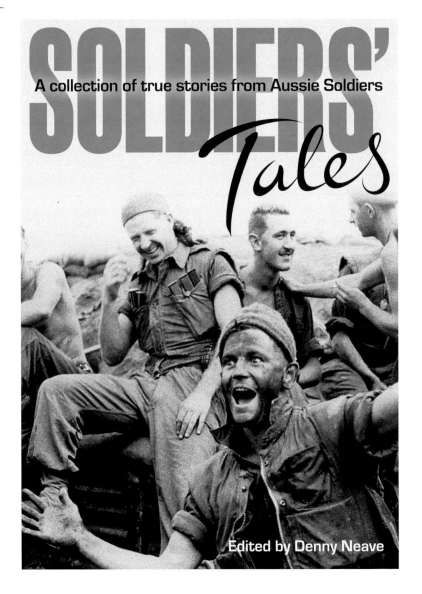

SOLDIERS' *Tales*

A collection of true stories from Aussie Soldiers

Edited by Denny Neave

View sample pages, reviews and more information
on this and other titles at www.bigskypublishing.com.au

BIG SKY PUBLISHING

"Plodding through mud up to the knees for days on end with a 25lb pack plus weapons and ammunition made me curse the war in no uncertain terms. Then one day I heard a soldier behind me praying, 'Dear God, help me pick up me feet, I'll put the bastards down'."

Captain Glenn Davidson, New Guinea, WWII

A collection of stories that are entertaining, emotional and humorous, Soldiers' Tales is a wonderful tribute to the Aussie Digger.

From World War One to the modern day conflict, Australian soldiers share their stories and anecdotes usually saved for Anzac Day or a catch-up with mates over a cup of tea or an icy cold beer.

In their own words they provide a fascinating glimpse of the many funny and touching moments that our Diggers often hold tight to their chest. The collection of stories featured in Soldiers' Tales vividly provide a taste of what a soldier's life is like in both war and peace.

From the pyramids of Egypt where a pint-sized Captain used lateral thinking to gain respect; Anzac day on the porch with Banjo; playing golf in Baghdad or a scorpion in the pants in Vietnam; their stories showcase the sense of humour and the importance of mateship to the Aussie digger.

Soldiers' Tales is a collection of yarns to warm the heart and bring a smile to your face or a tear to the eye. A wonderful collection of stories that will delight readers of all ages and linger on well after the book has been put aside.

Available at all good bookstores or purchase online at www.bigskypublishing.com.au
Postage within Australia is free. PO Box 303, Newport NSW 2106 Australia Ph: 1300 364 611

172

Aussie
SOLDIER
up close and personal

Denny Neave
with Craig Smith

View sample pages, reviews and more information
on this and other titles at www.bigskypublishing.com.au

"He is the raw steel whose spirit has been forged in the furnace of war from the Boer campaign and Gallipoli to the present day conflicts. It has hardened under fire in difficult situations during the desert and jungle campaigns of WW2, Korea, Borneo and Vietnam. It was then tempered under modern conflicts which have been far different, where compassion, understanding and patience are as much a part of the soldier's kitbag as his war fighting skills."

Warrant Officer Arthur Francis, CSC, OAM, ex-RSM Army

Compassion, Mateship, Courage, Initiative, Loyalty, Integrity and Trust.

These core values are the backbone of the soldier and are highlighted in the personal anecdotes and stories recounted in *Aussie Soldier up close and personal.*

From World War One to the modern day conflict, Australian soldiers young and old provide an up close and personal perspective on the Army's core values and how being a soldier is more then just putting on a uniform.

With anecdotes and excerpts from diaries that have never been published, plus stories and personal perspectives from the battle grounds of Europe, the jungles of New Guinea and Vietnam, the desert sands of Iraq, the complexities of Afghanistan as well as the peace keeping missions in Rwanda, Timor and Somalia, our soldiers' honest and thoughtful accounts run the gamut of emotions.

In addition *Aussie Soldier* includes stories about the Larrikin, Close Calls in Battle, extracts of Diaries and Letters as well as a Battle Book that summarises some of Australia's most famous battles.

Confronting, thoughtful and with a sense of humour the collection of stories featured in *Aussie Soldier* provide an insight into the human side of a high profile and often misconstrued field of expertise.

Available at all good bookstores or purchase online at www.bigskypublishing.com.au
Postage within Australia is free. PO Box 303, Newport NSW 2106 Australia Ph: 1300 364 611

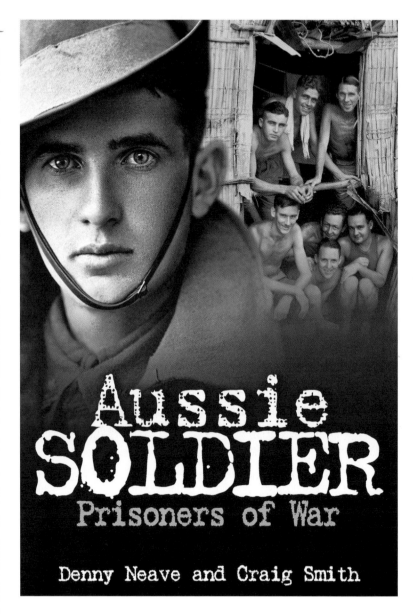

Aussie SOLDIER

Prisoners of War

Denny Neave and Craig Smith

View sample pages, reviews and more information
on this and other titles at www.bigskypublishing.com.au

BIG SKY PUBLISHING

"My experience as a POW definitely changed my outlook on life. It made me aware how precious life was, and how easily lost. I saw thousands of men's lives treated as rubbish by the Japanese. I survived the cholera outbreaks in Burma where you might say goodnight to the man lying next to you and find him dead beside you in the morning. I have valued each day since coming home. I know how lucky I am to have made it."

Private John "Jack" Thorpe, 105 Transport Platoon, Burma

Some 34,737 Australian service personnel were prisoners of war during the Boer War, World War I, World War II and the Korean War. Some lived to tell their story of survival through extreme hardship and to carry with them the burden of those who died. For many, their greatest victory would be in the simple act of surviving.

The courage of the thousands of men and women who served their country as POWs is integral to the Australian identity and history. Just as our national character was forged on the shores of Gallipoli, capture as a prisoner of war tested courage, defiance, mateship and required as much strength of character as any hard fought battle.

Aussie Soldier - Prisoners of War shares the voices of those who found themselves on the wrong side of the wire. It brings together an unforgettable collection of memories and experiences to be treasured as part of our military history.

These vivid and compelling stories show the extremes of war; the generosity of human nature and the cruelty, hate and indifference that human beings can inflict upon each other. The reminisces of our POW's will take you on their very personal journeys through capture, conditions, escape attempts, punishment, humour, keeping up morale and for those lucky enough, the taste of freedom.

Available at all good bookstores or purchase online at www.bigskypublishing.com.au
Postage within Australia is free. PO Box 303, Newport NSW 2106 Australia Ph: 1300 364 611

LONG TAN TO AFGHANISTAN DVD

Delta Company 6 RAR is warned for deployment to Afghanistan. The Company prepares for the tough training that lies ahead. A few travel to Vietnam to walk the battlefield of Long Tan — to walk in the footsteps of soldiers who served proudly and heroically. As their departure draws close, the men prepare those who will be left behind as best they can. But nothing can allay the concern of an anxious mother or a fearful wife — and the grief of a family whose son will not return.

This is the deeply personal story of soldiers preparing for battle and the anguished wait of loved ones at home from whom duty and service can demand the ultimate price.

Run time: 93 minutes

View sample pages, reviews and more information
on this and other titles at www.bigskypublishing.com.au